# Zinger
### and
# Me

# Zinger and Me

## Jack MacLeod

McClelland and Stewart

*The Canadian Publishers*
McClelland and Stewart Limited
25 Hollinger Road
Toronto M4B 3G2

Printed and bound in Canada


**CANADIAN CATALOGUING IN PUBLICATION DATA**

MacLeod, Jack.
  Zinger and me

ISBN 0-7710-5576-5

I. Title.

PS8575.L4587Z33   C813'.5'4   C79-094116-3
PR9199.3.M258Z33

*For Barbara*

"*In his letters, a man's soul lies naked.*"

Dr. Samuel Johnson

"*The archetypal activities of human society are all permeated with play.*"

Johan Huizinga, *Homo Ludens*

"*Most men are inclined, in their letters,*
*To rattle and shake at their fetters,*
  *To rage in the night*
  *And rail at their plight*
*And cock a few snooks at their betters.*"

Zinger

To: Spencer Tapsell
Chairman, Dept. of Economics
University of Saskatchewan
Saskatoon, Sask.

3 August 1976

Dear Spence,

They've done it again. The buggers have denied me tenure. It's a bloody outrage!

After luring me here with big talk and big promises, these bastards at Chiliast U. think they can walk all over me and leave me as Assistant Professor without tenure as long as they feel like it. To hell with that. Let me tell you, Spence, and you can tell them, that this cozy little clique of academic eunuchs have played sillybuggers once too often with the wrong boy, and this boy is going to tell them where they can stuff it. I DESERVE that promotion, and I intend to make one helluva fuss until I get it.

Do you realize that I've been teaching here since 1973? I've worked like a dog on my lectures, I've spent extra time with students, at least with some bright ones, and I've dutifully numbed my earnest ass on the chairs of innumerable committees in an attempt to "get along" and be a good fellow. Not once have I told our imbecile dean what I think of him. Talk about manful restraint! I haven't bad-mouthed the administration, disagreed with the Chairman, or even goosed the President's frolicsome little wife – not in public, anyway. And I'm a good teacher, dammit.

You've a very respectable reputation in the profession, Spence, and you've come through with references and testimonials on my behalf before. You must understand that I am being unfairly deprived and abused. I think some of the narrow "technicians" in the department, Chicago-school types all, resent my political views and my dabbling in what they call "Can-Kultchure." Fawk.

I beg you to intercede and to set the rascals straight, or to find me another opening.

In haste and in desperation,

J.T.

P.S.

Have you any news at all of Zinger? I have not seen him since last year, and he has not replied to my letters for months. Smig mentioned in a letter in July that Zinger was dragging ass a bit, that Chappie has left him, and that his employer, Dowie, no longer content with the usual game of firing him on Friday and re-hiring him on Monday, had recently retained a lawyer to find cause to have Zinger hanged. What has he done? What is he up to? I called him long distance last week, but got no answer. Here's the world going jauntily to hell in a handbasket and Zinger won't even answer his telephone. I can't stand it. Send me some good tidings instantly, if not sooner.

To:   J.T. McLaughlin,
      Assistant Professor

From:   L.T. Wright, Chairman,
        Department of Economics,
        Chiliast University
        Toronto

Date:   5 August 1976

MEMORANDUM:

This is to confirm our earlier conversation of 3 August. I regret that the vote of the tenure committee was negative.

However, the committee has recommended that in view of your previous professional experience in banking and in Ottawa, you should be granted an additional probationary period covered by a one year "sessional" contract. It is hoped that during the coming academic year you will be able to strengthen your publication record. I will ask the tenure committee to review your case within the next twelve months.

Good luck.

L.T.W.

From: Spencer Tapsell
Chairman, Dept. of Economics
University of Saskatchewan

J.T. Ol' Buddy,                                    6 August 1976

Now just calm down, boy, and let's sort out what the *real* situation is. I did try to help you land that job in the first place – although you were not "lured" into it, and I had to pull a few strings to get your name into consideration for the position. Certainly I will try to help you advance yourself. Count on me, but first, *inform* me. I'm not at all clear from your somewhat shrill and incoherent letter what is going on in Chiliast U. or why you were not promoted. You sound, if you'll pardon my saying so, just a trifle paranoid.

True, you did acquire some very interesting and useful experience in other lines before returning to the university. I think they gave you some credit for that in terms of salary if not in terms of academic rank. But this is a different league, you know, and a different game. Promotion is seldom an automatic thing in the scholarly community. The situation is probably more complex than you describe it, or than you want to believe. Years ago (1972?) you did tell me that you most particularly wanted to teach and that you were prepared to make sacrifices to get *out* of the Ottawa bureaucracy and into a professorial slot. You know that if I had an opening for you on our faculty I'd have been more than happy to have brought you back to Saskatoon, but you also know that we had no position open here at that time, certainly not in your specialty. Furthermore, you know that I wrote *glowing* letters of reference for you, perjuring myself as to what a sound and stable character you are, or might be, if you could find the right spot, and get it all together, and settle down to write some serious academic work. I still think you can. However, like a lot of your old friends here, I've been rather underwhelmed by your publication record since you became an assistant professor at Chiliast U.

What writing do you have in the works? You've bombarded me with Xerox copies and off-prints of various articles and minor squibs over the years, but what about a *serious* book? The name of the game, laddie, is publication. Writing page-seven comments and book reviews in the great grey and ghastly *Globe and Mail* is not what it's all about. I'd like to see, and I mean it in the most friendly manner, additional evidence of real research and more consequential scholarly publication, or at least more substantial work in progress, before I stick my neck out any further or write any more letters of recommendation for you. Our friendship over the years, since undergraduate days, is one thing, but before you go off half-cocked, or before I commit more solemn testimonials to paper, I'd like to have more information and *evidence* as to your current research and publications, or publications pending.

Tell you what. Here's what we should both do. You calm down, and stop being so raucously impatient about promotion and tenure, and reassure Patricia that she is not married to a failure in an academic dead end. You should both be of good cheer, and stop pressing so hard. Meanwhile, I'll take some careful soundings along the academic grapevine as to your status and your marketability at other universities, and at the same time you should send me an up-dated copy of your publication record and Curriculum Vitae, which I'll give very careful reconsideration. Possibly then I can offer more pointed advice.

As to Zinger. The last I heard from Prince Albert was that he did indeed get fired in July from his position as assistant editor of the P.A. *Northern Light*, but that Dowie relented and re-hired him before the month was out, although I'm at a loss to know why. Difficult to find a replacement, I guess. Chappie did leave him. She has filed for divorce and has found a job teaching high-school here in Saskatoon. *Grand* girl, Chappie. Why she put up with him for so long, I'll never know. But the by-line of Francis Z. Springer does keep re-appearing in the Prince Albert paper, so it seems that Zinger is still making a living, contrary to all reason and justice. Always was a bit of a loony, if you ask me.

Yours very sincerely,

Spence

To: Spencer Tapsell,
Chairman, Dept. of Economics
University of Saskatchewan

10 August 1977

Dear Spence,

I can't believe it. Calling me paranoid, yet. Bear in mind the nature of the gang of professorial thugs that surround me and you'll realize why I'm so upset.

Are you really going to lecture me about the rules of the academic game and deliver another sermon about publications? I ask you for help, and you pontificate about "consequential scholarly publications." Shit, Spence, I've got enough trouble.

For your prompt reply I do thank you, but if I wanted to be preached at I'd have trotted off to the Apostolic Mission. Merely because you are on the straight-and-narrow and a Chairman, while I am a lowly Assistant Professor scuffling for tenure, is no reason for you to pull rank on me and to come on all avuncular and piss-elegantly superior. You will recall, my portly friend, who helped you through Timmie's advanced theory class, and who it was in graduate school that showed you how to unravel some of the sticky points in your thesis. So knock it off with the sermons. I'm as good a teacher as you are any day, or better, and I've proved that I can hack it in the big bad world of the banks and the civil service while you were lollygagging around the university coffee lounges, and don't you forget it. Just because you are regarded as the leading expert in all northern Saskatchewan on some abstruse point of theory, have published the same dumb article on the Phillips Curve in nine different versions in nine different journals, and got promoted back in the days when such leap-frogging was easier, that's no reason to get huffy with me. Big deal. You're becoming broader of ass, Spence, but narrower of mind. I begin to suspect that, like some of my snooty colleagues here, you're actually jealous of my popularity with the students and my teaching ability, an ability which you pointedly did not mention in your letter.

I can just hear you, harrumphing and fulminating from the depths of your tub chair in the Faculty Club, with your fingers laced over your increasingly protruberant belly: "Yes, yes, of course Jesus Christ was a most competent teacher, but after all, what did he ever publish?"

Anyway, I am enclosing my most recent Curriculum Vitae as you suggested. Disregard my impatient tone. Do what you can. Give my very best to Smig, and to Timmie, and maybe you'd also show my C.V. to good old Gandy; he might have some useful views.

Regards,

J.T.

Enclosure to Spencer Tapsell

## Curriculum Vitae
## John T. McLaughlin

Born: 2 Oct. 1937, Regina, Saskatchewan.

Education:
- High School, Regina Central Collegiate, 1950–54
- B.A. (Honours), University of Saskatchewan, 1958
- M.A., London School of Economics, 1959
- Ph. D. (Econ.), Chiliast University, Toronto, 1965

   - thesis:The Influence of Veblen on Harold Innis and Canadian Economic Thought

Marital Status:
married, to the former Patricia E. Simpson (1964)

Dependants:
wife (see above), plus two children
Jocelyn H. McLaughlin, born 1965
Robby T. McLaughlin, born 1967
plus one Labrador Retriever, "Max"; voracious;
plus one first mortgage, at least equally voracious

Employment:
- construction labourer and truck driver, summers, 1954–'58
- junior economist, Sask. Economic Planning Board, summers of 1959 and 1960
- teaching assistant, econ., 1961–1963, Chiliast U.
- economic analyst, and assistant editor of "The Newsletter", Colonial Bank of Upper Canada, Bay St., Toronto, 1963–1967
- economist and staff writer, Royal Commission on Industrial Strategy, Ottawa, 1967–1968
- economist, Dept. of Finance, Govt. of Canada, 1968–1973

–Assistant Professor, Dept. of Economics, Chiliast U. (cross-appointed, Burke College), 1973 to present.

Publications:

–"Karl Polanyi and the Myth of Natural Markets", *Western Economic Quarterly*, Autumn, 1964
–"Walter Gordon: Economic Maverick", *Saturday Night*, July 1966
–"McLuhan's Indebtedness to Harold Innis", *Canadian Forum*, February 1967
–"Fixed Vs. Floating Exchange Rates", *Economica*, Fall, 1967
–"Thorstein Veblen: Social Iconoclast", *Canadian Forum*, December 1967
–Chapter 8, *Report of the Royal Commission on Industrial Strategy*, Queen's Printer, Ottawa, 1968, pp. 256-297.
–"Tommy Douglas: An Appreciation", *Canadian Forum*, August 1971
–"The Corporation: Master or Servant of the Market?", Saturday Night, *January 1974*
–"Corporate Concentration in Canada", *Journal of Canadian Studies*, Summer, 1974

Professional Associations:

Canadian Economics Association
Canadian Association of Business & Financial Analysts
American Economics Association
Committee for an Independent Canada
University League for Social Reform

Clubs:

Faculty Club, Chiliast University
Antique Automobile Club of Ontario
P.O.E.T.S. Corner, Bloor St. West Branch, Toronto

Hobbies:

Chess
Writing irreverent letters to the editor, to pseudo-intellectual twits, and to some perfect strangers.
Girl-watching and erotic fantasyzing.

To: Professor Jake Smigarowsky
Dept. of Political Science
University of Saskatchewan

11 August 1978

Dear Smig,

I have some problems of my own here at Chiliast U., involving tenure and the plentiful lack thereof for yours truly, as Spence may have mentioned to you. But I am very uneasy about Zinger, whose life seems to be in even worse shape than mine. He isn't much for replying to letters, and when I phone his house I get no answer. Your letter of July told me that the beauteous Margot Chapman Springer, whom I do acknowledge to be too good for the likes of Zinger, has left him. Chappie has hung in so marvellously for so long, and as we both know, living with Zinger isn't easy. Has she really thrown in the towel? Divorce? Is Chappie really going to be a high school teacher in Saskatoon?

Spence is being most extraordinarily owlish with me. His last letter was as plonking as a Rotary Club speech. I know he means well, and will come through in the end, but his increasing sanctimoniousness drives me up the wall. Does he have his eye on a university presidency, or the Senate, or ingratiating himself with Otto Lang for gawd's sake?

If you see Chappie, give her my love, no matter what her status may be as the former or estranged Mrs. Zinger, and if you have any news of that unlikely bastard, let me know.

Best regards,

J.T.

From: Spencer Tapsell
Chairman, Dept. of Economics
University of Saskatchewan

16 August 1976

J.T. Ol' Buddy,

I will disregard, for the sake of auld lang syne, your somewhat surly and intemperate response to my *well*-intentioned letter and my offer to be of assistance.

I have your C.V., and I must say that it reveals some considerable part of your problem. It is a *mess*. It is extremely ill-presented and flip, i.e., non-professional. It will not do.

You do go on about "teaching," don't you? Here's the bottom line: teaching is O.K., but publication *matters*.

Your curriculum vitae, you must understand, is of no little consequence in your presentation of self and your professional image in the scholarly community. Your C.V. is not at all satisfactory. Can you really be so naive?

First, as to dates. The proper chronological presentation of your career steps is important, and when you list "employment," you state what you were in fact doing at various times in your rather chaotic life, but you fail to lead with the significant dates first, and then follow with what you were doing between those dates. For example, you should list:

1968 – 1973: economist, Dept. of Finance, Ottawa
1973 – to present: Asst. Professor, Chiliast U.

And *spare* us the part about "construction labourer and truck driver," will you?

Furthermore, you've got to clean up your act and dump the somewhat adolescent attempts at humour re Hobbies and Clubs. You are not applying for an I.O.D.E. Fellowship or for membership in the York

Club, you know. Grow up. You sound as foolish as Zinger. And what, pray tell, is the P.O.E.T.S. Corner, anyway?? Nor are you the only academic in Canada with a dog or a mortgage. Don't be tiresome.

Most important, re your publications. It is not a particularly imposing list, but if this is all you've got to show for thirty-eight years of cudgelling your dull brain, at least your C.V. should present it better. For Pete's sake, soft-pedal the simple-minded journalism. Do not list the items from *Saturday Night* or even from the *Canadian Forum*. These do not cut any ice with scholars. You should have one category for "Miscellaneous Journalism" and another for articles in refereed academic journals. The trouble is, you appear to have only three items which managed to sneak past the referees of academically respectable publications: those in the *Western Economic Quarterly*, *Economica*, and *The Journal of Canadian Studies*, although the latter is a bit questionable. Your chapter in the Royal Commission *Report* should probably be listed separately, but because it was paid governmental hack work, it is not likely to win you many brownie points.

Also, you fail to include any section of "Work in Progress." This is where the crunch comes. Do you not have any work on the back burner, or any manuscripts in press or submitted to press, which could be listed to demonstrate that you are churning out goodies any minute, rather than lying fallow? You are so goddamn arrogant about most things, and yet you do not offer any foreshadowing of serious writing in progress.

Do you see what I mean? Your C.V. is too limp. Pull it, and yourself, together and suppress or discard some of the marginal items. If you are so sweaty to get tenure, you'll have to shape up.

I'll keep in touch.

Sincerely,

Spence

From: Francis Z. Springer
Prince Albert

16 Aug., '76

J.T.,

What have you got the wind up about this time? Betty says you phoned again last night and sounded in a dither, a state much favoured by academics, I gather. Do I owe you a letter or something?

The grapevine from Saskatoon informs me that you did not get tenure and might be heaved out. Doesn't surprise me. As that great philosopher Damon Runyon once said, "All life is six to five against."

Regards,

Zinger

To: Francis Z. Springer
Prince Albert

19 August 1976

Dear Zinger,

Who the hell is Betty? I thought you still had a wife, for kristsake, long suffering and presently apart as poor Chappie now seems to be. You really have given her a hard time over the years, and you know how warmly I feel about her. About young John, too. How is he taking this separation bit? Do you see him often? After the way you've ignored and mistreated your own family, Zinger, it throws me for a loop to phone you and find some strange female named Betty popping bubble-gum in my ear. What are you running there, a home for wayward teeny-boppers? A bordello? If you'd answer your phone, or return my calls, or at least reply to my letters with something less cryptic than Runyon's making book on the cosmic odds, I might begin to comprehend what in hell you're up to.

Do sit down and write me a proper letter. I worry about you, you turkey.

Very best,

J.T.

To: Spencer Tapsell,
Chairman, Dept. of Economics,
University of Saskatchewan

19 August 1976

Dear Spence,

I get your message. I read you loud and clear. As fate and good sense would have it, I am already hard at work on writing a "serious" piece, and am revising my thesis on Innis into book form. Having done that work for the Ph.D years ago, I thought it was all over with, but we all make mistakes, as the hedgehog said, climbing off the clothes-brush. If it is necessary for academic advancement, I will transform that exercise into a book and try hard to get it into print. I am burning the midnight oil, believe me. It should be ready to be submitted to the Press fairly soon. I'm trying, Spence, I'm trying!

As to the P.O.E.T.S. Corner, that is an acronym. Do you know what an acronym is, you staid bastard? When I was working for the Royal Commission in Ottawa, my boss the chairman was a singularly stunned S.O.B. One Friday, when we had just finished a good chapter (which said chairman was prepared to accept, but didn't at all understand), I told the boss that one of the staff was having a birthday and we were off for a rather long and liquid lunch. Would he like to join us? No, he said, no, he had a standing Friday noon appointment with his oldest friends at the P.O.E.T.S. Corner. I said, "I didn't know that you were a literary chap, or interested in poetry" – hell, I wasn't sure that the old fraud could READ. "It's not a poetry circle," he said, "it's an acronym. It stands for 'Piss on Everything, Tomorrow's Saturday.'" If you weren't so totally preoccupied with committees and being important, Smig or some of the other boys would have initiated you long ago.

But I do thank you for your interest, your advice and your help. Publish or perish, eh? Right. Gottcha. But what if I do both?

Regards,

J.T.

From: Jake Smigarowsky,
Dept. of Political Science
University of Saskatchewan

18 August 1976

Dear J.T.,

Just returned from holidays. Found Spence muttering about what an "ill-tempered ingrate" you are. He showed me your recent exchange of letters. Also have your note to me of the 11th. But one thing at a time, bucko.

Certainly am sorry that you did not get tenure. Be of good cheer. You may reach the dizzy heights of Associate Professor yet. Not entirely sure why you make such a big schtick of it all. You're still employed, aren't you? Thousands aren't. With tenure, plus a nickel, you can make a down payment on a thirty-five-cent cup of coffee.

Spence was much less than overjoyed about you snapping his garters. True, he seems inordinately pleased with himself since he became Chairman. His hat has shrunk a bit, or something. True, there is likely to be a Deanship open soon, and our solemn friend can scarcely wait to get his ample buttocks into a more plush Decanal chair. But don't be too hard on Spence. Even if he did not pursue the main chance, Muriel is the sort of pushy wife who would frog-march him into it anyway. She simply can't wait to put on a flowered hat and pour tea as Mrs. Dean. If you'd lived with a tight-assed broad like Muriel for fourteen years, you'd probably have made Dean yourself – or cut your wrists. She's so square that she thinks he is, and has persuaded Spence that he is a "major scholar." Muriel couldn't bring herself to say "shit" if she had a mouth full, and she probably thinks even the missionary position is "kinky."

Chappie, on the other hand – I enclose her new address – ah, Chappie is something else. Some tough broad, that, and some good. She split from P.A. and Zinger in July after what must have been one of the most epic battles since Vimy Ridge. Hot words were exchanged, and cold looks, plus some physical lumps as well as mutual offers to disembowel. More important, she has hired a lawyer and seems resolute. Pity. Zinger is impossible, of course, but I can't see where she's going to find another man half his size or another foeman worthy of her steel. Did you have the hots for her years ago? Zinger always thought you did. I wouldn't meddle if I were you, bucko.

But I do understand your concern about our journalist pal. From our first days together as undergrads, he was always very vivid. You knew him earlier, in high school, yes? And I guess you were always closest to him of any of us. When I meet people from our class of '58 it always seems to be Zinger that folks ask about first. Strange, because he keeps in touch with almost no one. Me, he is pleasant to, if I appear on his doorstep in Prince Albert, though I sometimes feel I'm being only tolerated. He does not show up in Saskatoon much. (I don't think he's been out of the province for five years.) A loner. So much so, I guess, that he doesn't seem to know or care that he's a loner. Oblivious. Self-sufficient. Clearly he has what we political scientists call "charisma," a plonking word which we use when we don't know quite how else to describe a guy who's got it. Like Churchill or Mao, like Mordecai Richler or Hemingway, Zinger doesn't – well, he doesn't REMIND you of anyone else. Solitary, but apparently happy. Probably that's it. He's happy. Or content. Or doesn't give a damn. Same thing. People like me and, I suspect, you, keep intruding on him, trying to sort out how the hell he can remain so imperturbable. Compared to Zinger, Diogenes was naive, La Rochfoucauld was an altruist, and Robinson Crusoe was a social butterfly.

You know, the more I think about this, and I've thought about Zinger's rare qualities before, the more I believe that he is less eccentric than people say, that he may be, if not the only "normal" person around, the least fussed or least fucked up guy we know. Here am I, and even ponderous Spence Tapsell, uneasy about your tenure situation, and you turning hand-springs about it, and Zinger is probably far more interested in why doorknobs turn to the right and not to the left, or what practical joke to play on Dowie next.

Yeh, here it is. Just rummaged around till I found this quote from
Ortega y Gasset:

> The man with the clear head is the man who looks life in the
> face, realizes that everything in it is problematic, and feels him-
> self lost. As this is the simple truth – that to live is to feel one-
> self lost – he who accepts it has already begun to find himself, to
> be on firm ground. Instinctively, as do the shipwrecked, he will
> look round for something to which to cling, and that tragic,
> ruthless glance, absolutely sincere, because it is the question of
> his salvation, will cause him to bring order into the chaos of his
> life. All the rest is rhetoric, posturing, farce. He who does not
> really feel himself lost, is lost without remission: that is to say,
> he never finds himself, never comes up against his own reality.

Glad I could find that. Shipwrecked. On the Saskatchewan prairie.

That, I suppose, is why Chappie chose him. Gawd knows he's
exasperating, but I guess he never bored her. And that is probably
why you and I find him so compulsively worth while.

Anyway, I must end this screed. Since you seem to share the general craving to learn what Zinger is up to, I can report the following:

Chappie is steering clear of him, and says she wouldn't even open
letters from him. Fact is, he never writes. Seldom phones. Young
John, now fifteen, is old enough to play it cool, and seems very level.
He goes up to Prince Albert by bus occasionally, and Zinger takes
him to movies or whorehouses or something.

Pay cheques have been erratic. Z. collected unemployment for two
weeks in July. Dowie warned him (again) in June when Zinger
slipped another limerick into the paper – you know how on Friday
afternoons he loves to slide some of his own doggerel into any empty
space on a page, or into the obituaries. The June effort, rather gentler
than his celebrated revival of "On the Bridge Stood the Bishop of
Buckingham," was:

There was a young lady from Exeter
So lovely that men craned their necks at her,
    The more obviously depraved
    Ostentatiously waved
Their distinguishing organs of sex at her.

Nothing grand, and worth only a passing chuckle at most in a high school paper, but when the Ladies Literary and Bird-Watching Society of West Heights sent an indignant letter to the editor, Dowie was not pleased. A small rocket went up. No further "offensive" filler appeared for a whole month.

Then in July two little items were observed by keen students of journalistic trivia. Tucked away in the "Business Personals" in a Friday edition, presumably after a meeting of the Prince Albert chapter of the P.O.E.T.S. Corner, was this terse item: "Mrs. Kojak is bald on both ends." In the same edition, on the Women's Page, the Helpful Hints for Happy Housewives column included some extra advice. "How to keep flies out of the kitchen: keep a crock of shit in the living room."

Dowie swallowed his cigar. Couldn't finger Z., though, because he couldn't prove authorship by the assistant editor. Next Monday, however, on a page for which Zinger is responsible, there appeared a story about a young couple, flying enthusiasts both, who were married in an airplane. The story was O.K. and the picture of the happy couple was fine, except that under the photo ran the short and simple cutline: "High Diddle Diddle."

Zinger was fired. No great sweat, though, because two weeks later he was back on the payroll. (I think it was the editor, good-hearted old Barney Hockley, who winkled him back on.) If God had wanted newspapers to be solemn, he shouldn't have invented journalists. He certainly shouldn't have invented Zinger.

And so to bed.

    Our love to Trisha,

        Smig

To: Jake Smigarowsky,
Dept. of Political Science
University of Saskatchewan

22 August 1976

Dear Smig,

Much thanks for your good letter. Glad to be informed about the situation, and I'm cheered by the realization that you are keeping in touch with Chappie and taking an interest in Zinger. My own preoccupations seem a little less burdensome when I think about this family civil war and about Mrs. Kojak.

Odd how even you find Z. so remarkable. People always have. Probably that is part of the difficulty. In high school his teachers kept telling him that he could do, or be, most anything he chose, because clearly he had the brains and the chutzpah. He could go far, they said. He could do things. He got very tired of hearing that, I think. Zinger never could discover anything he believed to be really worth doing. His mind turned more naturally to student pranks and adolescent capers. Never has changed much, I suppose. Even university seemed to bore him most of the time; certainly it never stretched him. The professors he found most interesting were the off-beat and rather quaint eccentrics. Gandy he liked, but did not entirely respect. Timmie he respected, but did not entirely like. Gandy once gave him a high A because of the "fresh vigour" of his writing in an essay, but Z. knew that the content of the paper was not worth the A. Timmie once gave him a B minus because she knew and said that he could do much better than what he handed in. He never forgave either one of them.

You knew him as an outsider and a cynic in university. In high school, as I look back on it, Zinger had already established his pattern: imagination, perversity, sloth, sensibility, outward gregariousness and popularity, but inward feelings of deep and bitter contempt for all who toed the orthodox lines.

And never on time. If he had a date at 8 p.m. he might (or might not) show up at 10:30. His teachers kept urging him to read, and read he did, but seldom to the end of a book, and still more seldom a text. He read English history, looking mainly for oddities and insights and good lines, I think. He read people like H.L. Mencken, Dorothy Parker, Fitzgerald, Alexander Woolcott, Santayana (he HATED Hemingway) and biographies. He once said to me, when I was in Grade 11 and he in grade 12 – we argued about this, as we argued loudly about most things – that he read biography to reassure himself that even "great" people didn't accomplish much, and that although he particularly enjoyed *The New Yorker* in those days, it convinced him that he never wanted to visit New York. He's been as good as his word on that, hasn't he? You mention that he hasn't been out of the province in five years. I think the fact is that he has never been further than Edmonton, and that he hasn't been across the Saskatchewan boundary for eighteen years.

From my own work, I recall a salty journalist once writing to Harold Innis that "what this country needs is a good five-cent bullshit filter." Zinger always had a bullshit filter built in. When we used to argue into the wee small hours, as adolescents do, the "meaning" of life and the "purpose" of life, Zinger once laconically observed that perhaps we were begging the question, that perhaps life had no meaning. I didn't know it then, and maybe he didn't either, but that was probably his first step, and mine, toward being an Existentialist. I think that conversation was in the winter of 195- – but it doesn't matter. Even then he had a face like a wounded eagle, or a forlorn Arab who'd just lost his last oil well. He had a keen and jagged cutting edge of astringent cynicism. He had, as the poet says, "eyes that gleamed like two rainbows over a ruined world," and rows and rows of girls wetting their pants over him. And he never seemed to notice. Plus ça change . . . .

What I'm trying to say, Smig, is thanks for your long and thoughtful letter, and thanks for keeping me in the picture. I'm pressing hard most nights, believe it or not, to write something more about Veblen and Innis, but I often think that I'm more interested in trying to figure out "why is Zinger?," my oldest friend, than what Innis had to tell us. Innis is a puzzle, but Zinger is an enigma. Innis is "challenging," as we say, but Zinger is threatening, because what sort of a world is it if you can't understand your best friend?

Well, I'll keep banging away at this tenure thing, and at my attempt to revise my old thesis into a book. May have to ask your advice about a number of points later.

Very best,

J.T.

P.S.

I guess one reason I find Zinger interesting is that he appeals to the anarchist streak of simple chaos which lurks in most of us. Because he wants so little, he has nearly everything and is content. Z. knows who he is, and where and what he is, and be damned to externals. He has dug his toes into his own soil and not gone helling after the elusive whores of ambition or pretence. Whereas we become restless, tightening ourselves up to jump through the hoops of academic orthodoxy and to run the race through the institutional rat-maze, Zinger remains a spectator, savouring his popcorn and his pocket flask in his seat in the bleachers, scratching himself and grinning at the spectacle. Having few hopes and fewer illusions, he is seldom disappointed and enjoys the show. Camus asks, can we imagine Sisyphus happy? Maybe. But can we imagine Sisyphus saying to hell with the Gods, leaning carelessly on the rock, laughing, and *not pushing*?

J.T.

From: Francis Z. Springer
Prince Albert

25 Aug., '76

J.T.,

Do keep a civil tongue in your head, old cock. You called Betty a "strange female." Tut-tut-fucking-tut. Strange she isn't; female she most emphatically is.

Strange she could not really be, because she doesn't have enough smarts. Doesn't have two brains to rub together. On the other hand, she does have a dynamite pair of charlies. These, when rubbed together, particularly with me or my appendage between them, do much to compensate for her lack of grey matter, and greatly enhance the quality of life around the old homestead.

As the kids say, "It's been lonely in the saddle since my horse died."

Things have been a bit bleak here. Don't worry about Chappie, though. She'll be back. It was just that over the years we seem to have developed an inconvenient variety of opinions concerning certain domestic fundamentals. Besides, I think she hates me. Not enough to stay away very long, though. This talk of teaching school in Saskatoon is all a ploy to induce me to run after her and beg her to come back. Not bloody likely. You know how I expect tranquillity and non-strife at my own poor hearthside. Poor – that's been a problem. But whatthehell. Just because, as the man said, life tends to be "solitary, poor, nasty, brutish and short" is no reason to be obsessed with money or position, and still less reason to go grovelling to wives in distant places. Solace and diversion can be found readily enough, it seems. It's all such shitteroo.

Chappie did put up a fair bit of shouting about my lack of ambition and my disinclination to leave P.A. Dead right. She got rather excessively snarky about it. One Sunday morning, after a somewhat brisk and intemperate exchange of views, I offered to brain her with the frying pan. She said, "I dare you," so of course I did. Bent hell out of the frying pan. Didn't seem to do her much good either. I recollect it was that same day that she packed up, took John, and stalked off down the road. She does incline to get uppity sometimes.

Since then I have had time for quiet reflection. I have ruminated fiercely on your situation and my own. I have concluded that life, my boy, Life is like a whoopee cushion. Just when you think you are comfortably ensconced, it farts and lets you down.

But the one who is strange is not my unfortunate and top-heavily snoobifferous friend Betty. The one who is strange, J.T., is you. You get into such flaps about tenure or whatever, and then get into a further snit about Chappie or me, writing anguished letters and phoning me at all hours. Such a fuss, and such a narcissistic fuss at that. Yes, narcissistic. A definition of a narcissist is, I believe, one who keeps shouting up his own arse-hole and listening for an echo. Don't kid the troops about being "worried" about me. You are merely worried that you don't understand some things which are really not your business and that you are too far away to give me sage fireside chats, ladling out great gorpy globs of academic advice that I don't want, being censorious about ol' Betty, and too far away in the mysterious east to meddle.

So don't.

Anyway, come up and see me some time, as the flagpole sitter said to Mae West. Or was it St. Peter who said that?

Whatever.

Regards,

Zinger

P.S.

On further reflection I have decided that life is not like a whoopee cushion. Life, in fact, is like a cucumber: round and sweet and green and verdant and tempting – and then some sonofabitch comes along and shoves it up your ass.

Z.

To: Margot Chapman Springer
Saskatoon

30 August 1976

Dear Chappie,

I got your new phone number from Smig, and I gather that decent scout is trying to look out for your interests. Lean on him if you need to. Smig is one of the best. Wish I were closer and could be some help. But I was glad to talk with you through Ma Bell the other night. Good to hear you sounding quick and sassy.

Seems as though John "The Bear" is staying level through your move and dislocation. Good kid, that, and I'm still proud that you and Zinger named him after me. As a Godfather, I'm too far away to be much use, but I enclose this book for John, Rostand's *Cyrano*, which he might be ready for. Tell him for me to keep his white plume waving; you too. Or as Dorothy Parker said,

> And though to good I never come,
> Inseparable my nose and thumb.

Hope your teaching job works out. I most earnestly wish that you and Zinger will be able to overcome your difficulties, and that neither of you will be excessively proud about taking the first step toward reconciliation. I don't need to tell you, Chappie, about his ego. If pride was made of feathers, Zinger could fly. He may not come pursuing you for a while. But keep the door open, right?

Let me know if I can do, or say, anything useful. Dammit, Chappie, I wish you'd get your pert ass back to Prince Albert. I wish, I really do hope – well, you know what I mean.

With fondness and optimism,

J.T.

From: Margot Chapman Springer
Saskatoon

6 September 1976

J.T. old dear,

I know you mean well, but you are off base. Thanks for your phone call and your letter and your concern, but if you think I'm going back to Zinger you've got rocks in your head. I'd cheerfully slice his balls off before I opened the door to that layabout louse ever again. I've had it.

He has sent Smig sniffing around to see whether I've "calmed down," and various others of our "friends" have come snuffling around to see whether they might offer me "consolation" and maybe get a quick and indulgent lay. But my draw-bridge is up, and my mind is firmly set and clear. I'll see Zinger fry in hell before I ever give him another civil word. The best years of my life, and all that, and more I cannot and will not give. Let him talk to the lawyer.

You won't believe this, but last weekend, just before school started, I actually swallowed hard and accompanied young John up to Prince Albert to see his father, and when I got there I found some cheap little bimbo with curlers in her hair making a casserole in MY kitchen. The place was a mess, a shambles, and this blank, vacant-eyed little twat was actually standing dripping cigarette ashes and mascara over my stove. As you know, and you've encouraged and winked at Zinger's numb torpor for years, I've had to take any number of sordid part-time jobs to keep enough money coming in. His salary has never been much; he has been fired by Dowie and lost pay-cheques so frequently that our finances have always been inadequate and chaotic. This little bimbo named Betty actually offered me coffee, asked me who I was, and suggested that Zinger "might" be home in an hour or two. I straightened the bitch out on a few fundamentals, I can tell you. I collected some clothes that I'd left behind, stormed through the place, tore up some of his shirts and shredded the living-room curtains, gouged a hole in his favourite poster of Diefenbaker, and offered pointed advice as I went out the door: "Remember," I shouted from the front steps, "remember, every time you kiss him, that I PAID FOR HIS TEETH!"

My lawyer will serve the papers. Keep your well-intentioned advice. I've been bled white, and I'm finished.

Yours indignantly,

Chappie

From: Spencer Tapsell
Chairman
Dept. of Economics
U. of Sask.

7 September 1976

J.T. Ol' Buddy,

That's more *like* it. Your letter of 19 August makes me feel much better about your professional position and your prospects. A book, eh? Revising your thesis is not *exactly* what I had in mind about "new work," but if you can turn that manuscript into a book and get it into print, your problems may be over. You do realize it takes some time to get a book into print, even when it is revised and finished, and you do understand that we of the scholarly community will want to look at the reviews of the resultant book by various authorities *before* we commit ourselves fully, but you are on the right track. Keep at it. A book in print would make all the difference.

I will of course be willing to give you a preliminary appraisal of the worth of any manuscript you produce. Certainly I could offer you, on the basis of my somewhat more extensive experience, suggestions for refinement. Probably you'll want me to write a Foreword or Introduction to the work, just to smooth your path toward critical acceptance. It will be my pleasure.

Getting on with writing is really much more constructive, J.T., than your previous yammering about "teaching." Your classroom performance cannot be reflected in your C.V. and cannot be measured in terms of refereed publications and column inches. The less said about students, I think, the better. If you go on and on about teaching, *serious* chaps will think you are merely an intellectual social worker, not a scholar.

Smig, I believe, is going up to Prince Albert soon to reinforce the tedious socialist gospel among the NDP faithful at some meeting or other. Doubtless he will be able to give you news of your reprobate friend Zinger. Personally I would be relieved never to see that rogue again. He is, if you ask me, increasingly a lush. When I last addressed the Prince Albert Rotary Club, on the subject of the Mackenzie Valley pipeline, he showed up no less than half drunk with a *most* unsavoury female person on his arm, and had the temerity to ask me whether the pipeline was in Canada's national interest or in the U.S. interest (as if there could be a difference), and then tried to read some preposterous poem about Indians and the musk ox. Interrupted the proceedings, you know. Musk oxen indeed. I think the woman with him was at least part musk ox. Zinger seems to me more amenable to musk than to reason. Pussy-whipped, I think. Chappie is well out of that.

Gandy, on the other hand, was also a subject of your recent inquiry. Good old skate, Gandy, but not an altogether serious chap. Increasingly frivolous, you realize, as he approaches retirement. The jolly tradition of the absent-minded professor is one thing, but Gandy's total abstraction is something else. Students say it's quite charming to see him meandering across the campus smiling benignly to himself about some half-remembered jest or other, but he may be, in fact, more than a little bonkers. He's always been a bit condescending to me, but I still talk with him just as though he were an equal, keeping up the old collegiality thing, you know. Last week I encountered him in the park by the riverside, near the Bessborough Hotel. I stopped and chatted with him briefly. At the end of our talk, he said to me, "By the way, Tapsell, when we met, was I walking toward the hotel, or walking away from it?" I assured him that he was walking toward the 25th Street Bridge, away from the Bess. "Oh good," he replied, "then I have *had* my lunch." What are you going to do with an old fool like that?

Sincerely,

Spence

From: Francis Z. Springer
Prince Albert

10 Sept., 1976

J.T.,

I gather you have been corresponding with Chappie. I wish you wouldn't. I gather that you have been offering her advice and encouragement. Don't. Leave it alone. Come and visit, and welcome, but do not interfere. Chappie's head is screwed up enough without you trying to play philosopher. You may be a good economist, but if we needed marital counselling I'd have written to Ann Landers.

Chappie is O.K. She is teaching and not starving. I am O.K. I seem to find stray girls, often young and pleasingly round, following me home from the beer parlours quite unbidden and quite willingly. My bed is not empty. I am not out of clean socks. Breakfast seems to get made, most days, whether by me boiling sausages and roasting Cornflakes, or by some nubile leftover from the previous night doing her thing and abusing the frozen kippers. No problem. Just an egg in a warm beer and we're off to work, hi-ho.

The problem is that so many well-intentioned but deadly people keep intruding and interfering. I've got enough of that, and enough is too much.

People are getting into my hair. I want to be left alone. You, above all others, should comprehend that. Things are less than perfect with me, but I decline to advertise, and I am much less than eager to listen to advice. Consider the words of Cicero: "He removes the greatest ornament of friendship who takes away from it respect."

Write me something cheerful.

May you drink cold and piss hot.

Zinger

From: Professor B.J. Gandy
Dept. of History
University of Saskatchewan

16 September 1976

My Dear McLaughlin,

Tapsell has been kind enough to inform me of your situation at Chiliast U. and to show me some of your recent exchange of epistles. I am pleased that you have seen fit to inquire of my opinions, however indirectly. Your group – Tapsell, Smigarowsky, Springer and yourself – always interested me because it was one of the ablest collections of prairie thistles since I taught Buckley, Cherry, and Teitelbaum in their graduating year. Teitelbaum remains Canada's best painter since the Group of Seven. And I recall reading a respectable essay of yours on Polanyi, as well as a short piece on T.C. Douglas; I do have some sense of your career since leaving Saskatoon even without Tapsell's waving your C.V. under my nose. He does tend to be somewhat brash and abrupt.

You will pardon my observing, McLaughlin, that I was informed of your apparent difficulties the day after Timmie slipped away, an event which may have coloured my views. Dear Timmie died quietly in her sleep. How fortunate. Should you become half the scholar that she was, your friends will be well satisfied.

You took at least two courses with Timmie, did you not? I wonder whether you ever fully appreciated her background. Remarkable woman. She did not, I must say, achieve tenure until she was rather older than you are now.

Mabel F. Timlin, you may not know, was born in Wisconsin in 1891. With $10 in financial assets at her disposal, she arrived in Saskatchewan in 1917 in search of work. After teaching English to other immigrants for a time, she became a clerk-typist in the Department of Agricultural Extension here at the university. Working at night, she completed her own B.A. in the late 1920s, and was placed in charge of the university's correspondence courses in 1929. Further details of her personal history might be almost incomprehensible to one of your generation; I will add only that she pursued graduate studies, one course at a time (usually in the summers) as her savings permitted through the depression of the thirties, achieving her doctorate in 1940 and an appointment at the rank of Assistant Professor (untenured) in that same year, at the age of forty-nine. From that time there flowed a steady stream of splendid publications in both theory and in applied economics which did not cease until well after her retirement in 1959. (Her pension was minuscule, but that did not diminish either her continued creativity or her cheeriness.)

Timmie always spoke well of you and your colleagues in the class of '58. She was the sort of teacher who always hoped that her students might do even better than she, and followed their careers with genuine interest. I am not entirely sure, however, that she would regard lack of tenure as an earth-shattering matter. Would she have been wrong?

I appreciate, as doubtless Timmie would have appreciated, that you are trying to be a good teacher. And well you should. In itself, however, that may not be enough. Substantial contributions to the mainstream of serious scholarship may also reasonably be expected. Tapsell, one gathers, has reminded you of the desirability of scholarly publication. Earnest young pup that he is, he is not wrong.

Teaching, I have observed in recent years, has become some kind of a fetish both with students and junior faculty. Overrated, I think. If we did not (mistakenly) try to teach too many unteachable mobs who are not much interested in the world of ideas to begin with, but restricted our attentions to the small intellectual elite, there would not be such a bothersome obsession with classroom performance.

I recall, with some satisfaction, that you and others of your year were not uncomplimentary about my lectures in British history. While pleasing, such flattery did not interest me. I always found that, at bottom, the nature or quality of what we laughingly call "teaching" does not much matter. Ninety per cent of the students are glad to be entertained, but because fundamentally they are not interested in ideas, they cannot greatly be helped by lectures. The other 10 per cent, perhaps equally pleased to be amused, cannot greatly be harmed, even by bad lectures, because they will read and think and take a genuine interest in their work even if the "teaching" one offers is less than edifying. I sometimes think that the more lucid the lectures, the less students read; the more you spoon-feed them with anecdoted and regimented points for notes of an a,b,c kind, the less likely they are to suffer the salutary pangs of mental indigestion, and therefore the less likely they are to think and inquire for themselves. Contemporary "student evaluations" of teaching performance, after all, would have graded Harold Innis as an unpopular and possibly incompetent instructor, but he (perhaps together with Frank Underhill) may have had a greater impact on generations of students than any other scholar.

I wonder, McLaughlin, whether as a classroom performer you may be in danger of pandering? After all, you are not, dear boy, in the entertainment business. Genuine scholarly activity is quite otherwise.

Frequently I receive phone calls from the CBC and other benighted "media" institutions inviting me to hold forth on "the future of Canada" or "Canadian-American relations" with two days' warning, or tomorrow morning. Absurd. Should I attempt to compete with the execrable Johnny Carson or even the amiable Peter Gzowski as a popular entertainer? A losing game at best, I should think, and often embarrassing. In show business, I believe, you are granted weeks if not months in which to rehearse, to perfect your "act," backed by batteries of writers and directors and research assistants and script girls, not to mention make-up artists and lighting technicians. But a professor, after years of education which leads him to understand (if nothing else) that the world is always more complicated and unpredictable than ordinary folks want to acknowledge, and after writing a Ph.D thesis or a book which may have taken three or four years to hone, is somehow expected to be as brief, witty, and dramatic as an actor or comedian, and on more serious and complex subjects, of course. Preposterous. And what I say about such performances on TV may apply equally to classroom "performance," might it not? Students, after all, want their teachers to rival Richard Burton, if not Dean Martin. Bullroar.

Ultimately, you have got to decide whether you are a scholar or in show business. We have, I fear, too many misguided colleagues who attempt both, and who fail at both, and bad luck to them. You could receive, of course, more social status and acclaim and remuneration in show business than in academia, but that is another story.

As to teaching – and I do comprehend your zeal to do well by students, a considerable quality to be sure – I think I can offer no better advice than to suggest that after forty years of practising the art, I'm not sure how to teach. No one seems certain how best to teach, or how to teach teachers – which is why colleges of education are usually such jokes and sloughs of incompetence. Possibly you might find useful my own four rules for teaching, which are all I've had to go by all these years:

1. Try to persuade students to read, to read books.

2. Try to *tempt* students to read books.

3. Try to communicate concern for your subject, and respect for your subject, or even (on good days) enthusiasm.

4. Before entering the lecture hall, always check your fly.

Forgive me for scribbling on at such length, dear boy, but now that I am so close to retirement I can at least indulge myself in the luxury of full expression. And I do wish you well.

Yours very sincerely,

B.J. Gandy

From: Jake Smigarowsky
Dept. Pol. Sci.,
University of Sask.

17 September 1976

Dear J.T.

When I was in Prince Albert the other day I heard about a kafuffle at the local Rotary Club which mildly entertained some of the citizenry and involved two of our friends, bucko. Spence Tapsell, as the invited speaker, held forth on how the Mackenzie Valley pipeline project would help to develop northern resources and benefit Canada. Questions from the floor probed Spence as to why Canadian banks wanted to finance a pipeline from Alaska to south of the 49th Parallel, and why those Canadian banks wanted a government guarantee of their money from Ottawa. If the Yankees wanted it, why didn't they finance the project, and what was in it for us? Was our environment being raped for foreign benefit?

Spence began to flounder. The less certain he is, the more he tends to huff and puff. Then he spied a friend, or someone he thought might be a friend, none other than Prince Albert's own Pulitzer Prize aspirant, Francis Z. Springer. This worthy, covering the event for the *Northern Light*, hiccupped a hostile question concerning the rights of the native people, and then launched into a passionate declamation of doggerel concerning eagles and musk oxen which went, I'm told, as follows:

> A very strange critter, the eagle,
> Who preys on the beaver and beagle,
>   Feeding on lesser friends,
>   Then ultimately ends
> Being fat at expense of the feeble.

> But the musk ox is not one of them who can
> Be an endless exporter of pemmican,
>> Depleting his sources
>> Of flesh and resources
> Costs his'n, and benefits American.

The meeting broke up in confusion at about that point. Zinger weaved his way unsteadily back to the office, and Spence had to be physically restrained from going after him with an axe.

During my visit, I was able to spend a few convivial hours with our journalist friend. While hoisting a tankard or two in a bar he acquired, God knows how, two young ladies (do journalists have groupies?) who were more than willing to accompany us back to Zinger's place. One of them was still there when I left next morning. Since Chappie's departure, Zinger has lived off and on with a succulent succession of girls who were each enjoyed until he became conscious that he might be being intruded upon, that they were putting clothes into the closet, and bringing more than toothbrushes with them. Then, they got shoved out. The trouble is, young girls seem to have distinctly limited capacities for booze and for conversation past 3:00 A.M., and tendencies to settle in. Zinger needs diversion, certainly, but more urgently he seems to require dedicated drinkers and companions who can help him through the long dark hours of dismay when the night is black and the ravens croak.

He carouses. He is not without company. But I think he is very much alone.

I don't envy him.

Smig

From: Spencer Tapsell
Dept. of Economics
University of Sask.

19 September 1976

J.T. Ol' Buddy,

The grapevine tells me that there is *likely* to be an opening at a fairly senior level in the Department of Economics at Lethbridge University for next year. Would you be interested in Lethbridge? The slot would be for either associate or full professor, *with* tenure. The post has not yet been advertised, and with the academic job market the way it is, there may be numerous applicants, but I'd be glad to suggest your name to the chairman there.

Have you cleaned up your C.V. yet? If so, you might send one along.

Sincerely,

Spence

To: Spencer Tapsell
U. of Sask.
Saskatoon

22 September 1976

Dear Spence,

Thanks a lot, but no thanks. I would NOT be interested in Leth-bridge. Frankly, I like to think that I'm beyond begging for a slot like that.

Do you remember the story of the very famous actor who, while "between engagements," was offered a small part, much smaller than he would normally play? He was assured that the part would not take much of his time. He said no. He was assured that he'd receive good billing, just under the lead. He said no. He was assured that his fee would be high, top dollar per hour. Again, no. "Look," said his agent, "if your hang-up is not time, or billing, or even money, why won't you do it?" "Because," said the actor, "I'm too fucking grand."

Lethbridge is a nice place, but it's not for me. I've decided that I'm going to make it here in the big town, at Chiliast U., or not at all. I'm going to get tenure, Spence, and I'm going to get it here.

For several months now – since mid-summer, when I first realized that the tenure decision might be negative this year – I've been slug-ging away at the revision of my Ph.D thesis for publication. I think the manuscript is in pretty fair shape at this point, and I have a typist cranking it out. I also have an article coming out in the *Canadian Forum* very soon, and my friend Cutty Cuttshaw and I are collabo-rating on a textbook project, a Reader. With a few course adoptions, an anthology like this might make a few bucks in royalties, as well as fill out my list of publications. So I do have "Work in Progress" which may warm your cold academic heart, and I do expect to de-liver the book manuscript on Veblen-Innis to the Press very shortly.

I'm bearing down, by Gawd, and I'm going to give it one helluva shot.

Thanks anyway,

J.T.

From: Francis Z. Springer
Prince Albert

23 Sept., '76

J.T.,

It is after midnight and I can't sleep. Betty, who seemed to cause you such consternation, is long gone. So are several of her successors. Easy come, easy departure, I always say.

It has been interesting to me to discover that the world is full of hungry if not desperate females who will take up with any old stick like me in search of a male, any male, and a little companionship. Do you remember how difficult it was for us to get laid in the 1950s? Every mother's daughter was uptight about getting pregnant, and had been drilled in the iron discipline of keeping her legs together. If I ever write my autobiography, volume one will be called, "My First 25 Years with an Erection," or "What Do You Say After You've Said Thanks for the Hand Job?" How long ago it all seems. Now, since the pill and the sexual revolution, and since it became O.K. to be queer, what to my wondering eyes should appear but an endless parade of available pussy. It seems to follow me home many nights. What a good joke that the shoe is now on the other foot. The sexual revolution was supposed to liberate women. Not bloody likely. All it did was make women more "available," and frighten a lot of men.

After I spent my formative years with a stiff prick and nowhere to put it, the spinning world now reveals that almost any unmarried female over 25, and not a few of the marrieds, are trying harder to get men than we tried for a good night kiss in high school. Seems to me strange, but there just aren't any men around who are over 25 and single. Where did they all go? Why am I surrounded by cooze? Is it different in Toronto?

This is a whole new world to me. I think I like it. "Meaningful relationships" are still what they talk about, but now that the girls are accustomed to being turned upside down for the price of a dinner, it's a new ball game. I used to wonder whether I could make the team, and here I am with the only bat in town. When Chappie left, I worried whether I'd have – well, difficulties. Unh, unh. On the contrary, I find that most women now are (compared to the frigid fifties) nymphomaniacs, a nympho being defined as a female who'll do it after having had her hair done.

Tapsell made an ass of himself here recently preaching subservience to American economic domination. As the man said, I've tried him drunk and I've tried him sober, and there's nothing in him. He is rapidly becoming a rotund caricature of himself. Smig, who later addressed the local NDP faithful on the economic evils of the 1930s, was not much better. The world has changed. Such a right-wing backlash. Good left-liberals and card-carrying NDPers of yesteryear are now baying about the evils of immigration and lusting for a return to capital punishment. Public hangings might prove entertaining, and personally I have my own little list, but that's not my idea of social progress.

Meanwhile, back in the realm of friendship and civility, which is all we have left in a mad world, Smig and I passed a diverting and convivial evening together last week. He wears well, and for an intellectual he's not entirely foolish. However, I believe that Smig is telling anyone who will listen in Saskatoon, notably including Chappie, that I am a satyr, a dirty old man who relentlessly pursues virgins. Not so; I merely attempt to deal with what turns up, or turns over. Sometimes it's boring. Still, it helps to pass the time.

But we must seize life by the short and curly. *Coito, ergo sum* is my new motto, and never look a gift cunt in the clitoris.

Yours wearily,

Zinger

P.S.

Send me more newspaper clippings. I get the *Globe and Mail* a day late, but there must be something else happening in the eastern newspapers. Doug Fisher? Richard Gwyn? Most of our pundits seem so sure of what is going on this week, and then change direction next week. They all seem so certain, and then turn somersaults to rationalize why they were wrong. British and even some American journalists, I think, are both more tentative and more steady, ready to criticize, but less parochial and pontifical, much less creatures of whim and political fashion. Canadian journalism seems to me excessively faddish. Does no one have any convictions, any base-points or principles? I have been rereading Gibbon, and reading Marcus Aurelius. Let me know what you think about God, life, love, destiny, and all that shitteroo.

Z.

To: Francis Z. Springer
Prince Albert

26 September 1976

Dear Zinger,

Yeah. How right you are. With a few honourable exceptions such as my friend Cuttshaw, the Faculty Club and the coffee lounges here are always buffetted by transient gusts of journalistic opinion. The trouble with Canada is that we have too many mainsails, ready to tack with every shift of political wind, and too few rudders. Even important scholars such as Underhill and Forsey, having been founders of the CCF, ended up as Liberal apologists. The same paparazzi who creamed over Trudeau in '68 condemn him in '76 for doing and saying the same things he did before with the same shrug, the same style. Styles and fashions change, but the problems don't.

How often do you write editorials for the *Northern Light*? Why not send some along to me? Here in the east, western opinion is hard to fathom. Separatism is not merely an English-French phenomenon, I think, but a more general failure to read each other on an east-west axis. Everybody in Toronto can tell you what the prevailing view is in Washington or New York, but opinion in Calgary or Halifax remains mysterious. None of this would have happened if the CBC had existed. Whatever became of the CBC, that great vehicle of national unity, that splendid "alternative" to broadcasting with commercials? When they get around to writing the history of good ideas gone sour in Canada, surely the longest chapter will be on the CBC.

As for me, these days (and nights) I'm working my butt off at the typewriter. I'm spending less time jawing with students. Gandy, by the way, gave me a heavy shot in a recent communication. He made me pause and gulp a bit. I'll enclose his letter; it might interest you, not least because it tells a lot about the late lamented Timmie.

Timmie is gone. What a grand person she was. Makes you think.

None of us is an adolescent any longer, though I've often gathered from Gandy and other white-thatched old tigers that inside each octogenarian there persists the spirit of a ten-year-old.

But Zinger, soon I will be thirty-nine – next month, in fact. I mean, THIRTY-NINE! Almost forty, for kristsake; no longer young. The game is more than half over and I feel I'm just beginning. Whatever happened to twenty-nine?? As we slide down the slippery slopes to senility, I don't even have the assurance of a steady job. What I do have is thinning hair, thickening waist, receding gums, halitosis, and terminal dandruff. Where did we misplace youth and spring and panty-raids? I still feel young, dammit, and juicy, but I have begun to notice that my students regard me as "different," an object of historical curiosity. They inquire, respectfully, whether I ever met Diefenbaker and somehow convey the impression that they wouldn't be surprised if I'd shaken hands with Moses. Put 'er there, Mo, and let me carry that tablet for you. I don't FEEL "different." I have the same eager and needy spirit inside, here, where I live, as I had at nineteen. But I guess jean-suits don't seem right on me any more. There you are, screwing your way through the finest of Prince Albert's womanhood. Here am I, churning out pages in desperate haste and attempting to guide nineteen-year-olds into adult society. Yet suddenly I sense that I am regarded by my students as a mission-ary from the aged rather than their emissary to the aged.

Old. My Gawd, Zinger, I wonder if the game is not up, whether I'm not obsolete before I had time to learn the rules and get started?

You, I suppose, in effect, having "retired" from the big game in the big world to the rustic tranquillity of your northern fun-house shortly after graduation, still reside in the ageless and fanciful realm of the practical joke. How do you keep it up, oh guru of the north, and how do you get it up?

Sorry, Z., I'm just feeling bleak and forlorn tonight. Here it is past 1:00 A.M. Most nights I bang the typewriter and my head against the wall, from about 7:30 till midnight, trying to whip this miserable manuscript on Innis into shape. I chain-smoke, and the level in the scotch bottle keeps descending as I pursue the ideas down the page.

Rather too heavily into the bottle, I'm afraid. Sometimes at the end of a night like this the stairs seem to shift under my feet as I stumble up to my fartsack. Have just one more before lights-out, J.T.? Thanks, I think I will. Stephen Leacock's lines keep recurring to me: "Writing is no problem. You merely jot down the ideas as they occur to you. Now, the jotting down is simplicity itself. But the occurring, ah, that's difficult."

If there's anything in the world as difficult as writing, it must be editing and revising and rewriting. I keep making outlines and revised guidelines for the framework of my argument, and trying to stick to them, but invariably as I grind out the paragraphs new and unexpected side-tracks and sub-themes keep appearing, new doors keep opening in what I thought were solid walls. Veblen is O.K., but with Innis astonishing geysers of ideas keep spurting up through the weak mesh of my outline. The sting of his insights and intuitions keeps pushing my crayon over the lines in my colouring book. His ideas and his very convoluted sentences won't hold still. Damnably wiggly and formless, those sentences. I have great trouble nailing them to the page. Well, Jello isn't very solid either, but they sell a helluva lot of it. Maybe there's hope.

What about your own efforts, Zinger? Are you writing anything besides those ineluctable editorials and the local news? Smig and I always thought that you were the "natural" among those of us who ever tried to write. Anything happening on your pages?

Send me some paragraphs and a birthday card, or a gross of Geritol.

And keep your pecker up.

J.T.

From: Spencer Tapsell
Dept. of Economics
University of Saskatchewan

26 September 1976

J.T. Ol' Buddy,

You dumb sonofabitch, I was not trying to get you a *job* in Lethbridge. I was trying to get you an *offer* from Lethbridge, an offer that you could use as evidence of your marketability, that you could use as a *lever* on your Chairman or Dean. A solid offer would help to establish your *bona fides*, you jerk, and if you don't understand that, you don't understand the rules of the academic game. Aren't you *serious* about this at all? I don't know why I bother. I keep trying to provide you with live ammunition for job warfare, and you keep on playing squirt guns.

Well, up yours with a water pistol, and lots of luck. You'll need it. For your sake I hope you get your book on Innis into print quickly or else you may find yourself dead on the floor of the job market.

Another squib coming out in the *Canadian Forum*, eh? I'm laughing. You've really got to stop wasting your time on the journalistic kick. That's O.K. for a sideline and funzies, but it will not cut any ice at all with a tenure committee. And please, don't hand me any of that crap about collaborating with Cuttshaw on an anthology. Another collection of "readings," yet. Who needs it? Listen, an anthology is a non-book. They're a drug on the market, and there are no academic Brownie points to be earned that way. To the making of books there is no end, and to the making of non-books there is no point. Tell Cutty for me that you should both forget it.

Yours, etc.,

Spencer T.

To: Spencer Tapsell
U. of Sask.

29 September 1976

Dear Mr. Chairman Your Honour Sir,

All right, Spence, all right. I get your message. You are a devious game-playing bastard. Thanks again, but no thanks. Lethbridge is a nice place; there are some good people there, and if you think I'm ready to stoop so low as to try to diddle with offers or to beg for offers that wouldn't be taken seriously, then you're full of shit.

As for your sermons about writing occasionally for non-academic journals, your patronizing remarks about "non-books," and your snide predictions concerning my imminent academic demise, I'll add only this: I wish you had become a Bishop instead of a pretentious departmental chairman, because then you'd only want me to kiss your ring.

And this boy ain't about to do any more stooping or kissing.

Same to you, fella.

J.T.

From: Francis Z. Springer
Prince Albert

30 Sept., '76

J.T.,

Your somewhat gooey letter arrived this morning. In one way it warmed my heart to hear from you and to learn more about your arcane labours. Nice, too, that you could get through one entire letter without scolding me about the female of the species – is this a record? In another way I found your elaborate progress report sad, and would have wept a salty tear for you if you were not already awash in a great tearful sea of self-pity. Brace up. You are not the only person alive who has ever had to struggle with writing and wrassle with sentences, or even with convoluted Innisian pronouncements. "What big sentences you have, Grandma." "All the better to bamboozle you with, child." If the old gorgonzola had been able to think in a straight line he wouldn't have written such circular sentences which chase their own tails. Take it from me, as an old tail chaser. And if you can't stand the stink, stay out of the abbatoir.

So it's 39, is it, and the big four-oh not far away? Shit, lad, you forget that the bold P.A. flash is two years older than you. I've passed the 40 mark and it doesn't hurt a bit. The trick is not to look back over your shoulder; something might be gaining on you. Lay on, MacDuff, and damned be he who first cries "Hold, we've run out of ice cubes."

Yes, I still push my pen across the paper wastelands, particularly in the dead of night. Like you, apparently, I keep a bottle near my elbow as defence against the dreads. Unlike you, however, I do not kid myself that my paragraphs are destined to win plaudits or Pulitzers. I still write a snappy intro, but I'm less brisk in dealing with middles, and have never yet been able to reach a point where I had to worry about polishing a wrap. I may never finish anything. Whatthehell. Conclusions are not my strong point. But I'm hell for openers.

Recently I bought a desk. It's a solid desk of some dignity, a good companion, and doesn't cost much to feed. Found it in the bowels of the *Northern Light* building behind some packing cases, and persuaded Dowie to let me take it home for 20 bucks. That ignoramus didn't realize how old it is. It's oak, a marvellous elderly roll-top, and was probably in use when Louis Riel was still running around goosing buffalo with his crucifix. (I like almost everything antique, except women.) Sometimes I feel like crawling into it, assuming the foetal position, and rolling the top down forever. More often I sit at my desk and contemplate life's little insupportabilities. With my feet up I savour my fleeting petty victories. I smart over past humiliations and defeats and confidently await the new. In contrast to your frantic clawing at the typewriter, trying to please god knows what learned jury of three-cornered academic assholes, I attempt only a few leisurely scribblings of things that I think are nice. When I leave the office I transcend deadlines by having none. I produce a few fugitive poems whether the world needs them or not, plus some furtive limericks to tuck away into the Women's Page when Dowie isn't looking. My life these days seems so insignificant, feckless and futile that my midnight cantos afford me great pleasure.

Actually, Dowie isn't my major problem of late. It's Barney. When Dowie as publisher fires me for some real or imaginary peccadillo, as he seems to have some deep-rooted and perverse compulsion to do every so often, it is Barney Hockley who stealthily re-hires me. As editor, and with all his seniority, Barney knows how to circumnavigate his forgetful publisher. Barney is also an old crony of the mayor and of Dief, which doesn't hurt. Hockley just plods along very carefully. He has an ulcer, and breath that could knock a buzzard off a shit wagon at 40 paces. He just wants to get the pages out with a minimum of fuss. As for news and scoops, he couldn't find his own ass with both hands. And lazy. Barney is so lazy that his idea of masturbation is to stick his dork into the ground and wait for an earthquake. That's where I come in; not in making the earth move for him, Mrs. Hemingway, but in keeping the editorial desk firm.

I've acquired the lambent knack of extruding turgid editorial prose fairly quickly by the broad linear yard. Not a major skill, but a trick much prized by idle senior editors. Therefore, Barney likes me. More important, Barney re-hires me. By our mutual nonexertions, we each do our bit to keep the other on the payroll and the local unemployment figures reduced by one. So long as he keeps Dowie placated, I keep the presses rolling. As soon as I feel Dowie's wrath rising or the fetid breath of Barney behind me, I snap-to like a Pavlovian dog and emit another vacuous but resounding screed on patriation of the constitution or the socio-economic problems of Lower Somaliland. Nobody reads them anyway. Except for other equally cynical and lame-brained editorial con men, that is, who reprint them on off days to fill up gaping holes in their own papers in other towns, and thus do we all constructively influence the ineffable course of public affairs. It's all bullshitteroo.

As the Pope said, when asked if he found his Holy Eminence satisfactory, "Ech, it's a living."

Let's see, where were we? Deep into aging and writing, I think. You'll remember that, like every other semi-literate hack in the west, I'd begun a book years ago on the Riel Rebellion. After scrabbling around for a time it seemed to me that Gabriel Dumont might be more interesting than Riel, so I snuffled along that trail for a while. Happily George Woodcock's most excellent book on Dumont appeared (have you read it?) and enabled me to back off and retire gracefully. I have tried, in my time, to be an historian, but sloth and self-doubt keep deflecting me. Apart from prostitution and maybe the art of the ecdysiast – stripteaser to you, dolt – there is probably no calling that is not better practised by the professional than by the amateur. I never could see myself as a professional. But as my amateur passions occasionally seize me, I still dabble with a never-to-be-completed work on the limerick as an art form, an 11-volume opus on the history of the crossword puzzle, and the beguiling possibilities of writing a stentorian drama about Mr. Diefenbaker, bless him. However, most of the gestures I make as a paragrapher, like my own squalid existence, seem to begin as high tragedy and rapidly decline into low farce. And so it goes.

As to aging and your apparent menopausal recession, be of good cheer. It'll all get worse, and whatthehell. I curse and rant and rail. Loudly do I declaim upon the daunting vicissitudes of fortune and the imponderable inconstancy of women, notably Chappie. I bellow and rage in the night and hurl candlesticks through the window at errant moonbeams. I drink. I ruminate and noctambulate. I make model airplanes. If middle age comes, can second childhood be far behind?

But don't you crack up, old friend. I swear I don't know why you want to do what you do or what the point is to all your tippy-toe academic footwork. But hang in there, daddy. In a peculiar way, you are one of the few fixed points in my whirling world. Don't let the buggers get you down.

On the evening of your birthday I will lift a glass, face the east, and propose a toast. And listen for an echo.

Cheers.

Zinger

P.S.

To commemorate this lugubrious exchange of jottings I have composed a sonnet.

> A surly old man with a scythe
> Reaps souls as the ultimate tithe;
>    Quoth I, don't reap mine,
>    Much later'd be fine,
> Let me meanwhile persist being blythe.

Curious how my sonnets tend to depart from the standard form.

Whatever.

Z.

P.P.S.

What I can't figure is why you want to get tenure at all. Such a fuss. If you get it, you'll be stuck, and stuck in the evil east at that. It's incomprefuckinghensible to me. Tenure isn't a prize, it's a trap. Do you think Bertrand Russell ever had tenure? Or Marx or Vonnegut or Charlie Chaplin? If you get it, you'll be lock-stepping in the academic chain gang forever, and may never have the balls to quit or experiment or emit a raw bellow again. You used to be a good western coyote, and now you want to be a tame eastern lap dog.

Zing it.

Z.

From: Mother
Regina, Sask.

30 September 1976

John Dear,

Happy Birthday, son. I hope you are well. Tell little Robby to look after his sniffles. What grades are Robby and Jocelyn in at school this year? It's so hard to keep track. I'm sure I don't know what good school is anymore anyway. The children around here all seem so noisy and ill-mannered, and carry transistor radios around with them or slouch in front of a TV set. There's nothing much good on TV these days, is there, except Father and I like "Headline Hunters" and "Front Page Challenge," apart from that rude Mr. Sinclair. I'm not sure that I understood you on the phone last night, talking about your work. Are you going to leave the university, dear, and look for a real job? That would be nice. Probably you will enjoy that, and Dad says you'll get rid of your radical ideas and bring home a larger paycheck. That would be nice, too. Your Father hasn't been at all well lately. He still has those pains in his leg and hip and he's been coming home from work early. So I have to make dinner early. Anyway he hasn't been up to his usual self lately. Your odd friend Mr. Smigarowsky was in Regina last weekend and dropped in on us (the house looked a fright, but I'm sure *he* wouldn't mind) and had a long chat with Dad. They seemed to find something to chat about, I'm sure I don't know what. Mr. Smigarowsky (is it Dr.??) seems to be very nice for one of those people, and isn't it clever of a Ukaranian to become a professor just like you and Dr. Gandy? Do write to your Father, dear. We're both so proud of you. Anyway, I'm sending you a little gift and some baking by the next delivery. Give our love to Robby and Jocelyn and say hello to Patricia also.

Love,
Mother

To: Professor Jake Smigarowsky
Department of Political Science
University of Saskatchewan

3 October 1976

Dear Smig,

I saw your article on Regulatory Agencies in the Journal last week. Congrats on its appearance. I found it very interesting, and even useful. Assigned it to my fourth year class; if you should get to Toronto any time this term or next, I hope you might come and talk to them about it. Doubtless I could get Trish to feed you a dinner as partial recompense for your trouble. It would be good to see you.

My sainted mother reports that you were kind enough to drop in on them when you were last in Regina. I want to thank you for that. Dad thinks particularly well of you, and I know he enjoys your company. Did he offer you any of his homemade hooch or his Saskatoonberry wine? That's his way of showing affection, believe it or not. Almost his only way, except with my kids. He's very good with Jossy and Robby, and they think the world of him. Dad's homemade wine will rot your socks if you're not careful. It has been known to strike terror into the hearts of stronger men than you, and one sip could pucker the lips of a plastic Ubangi. Dad says you're "very level-headed for a professor," his highest accolade, and even Mom allows as how you're not such a bad guy for a Bohunk. Tell her that Ruth is a Presbyterian, and you might become acceptable. Mom keeps asking me to write to Dad, but I never know what to say to him. Cranky old walrus. He keeps complaining of a glitch in his leg and a pain in his hip, but it's probably nothing serious, do you think?

I'm near the end of a long, long road with my Innis manuscript and look forward to a vast blowout when I finally ship it off to the Press. Trish says if I mention Innis or tenure to her one more time she'll scream. The crashing irony of it all is that when I got the Ph.D back in '65 I took my only copy of the goddam thesis and made a ceremonial bonfire of it and never wanted to see it again. Couldn't even bring myself to read it. Fear and loathing on the doctoral trail. But such are the grubby twists of fate and the tenure committee that this summer I had to haul my ass to the library, get a copy out of the dusty stacks, and make a Xerox copy to work from. Not much fun, but I'll have some good stories to tell when next I get to a meeting of the P.O.E.T.S. Corner. Won't be long now.

Can it be that our fat friend Tapsell is flipping out? Possibly you know that he seriously proposed to me some dirty diddle re trying to get a job offer from Lethbridge so that I could use it as a club against my own department. Jeez. Maybe I should have given him a bigger blast. I merely explained my views to him, with restraint. "Go fuck yourself, Tapsell," I explained calmly. That's not really how anyone would play the game of academic musical chairs, is it Smig? I left the bank and the civil service in order to avoid exactly that sort of thing.

Anyway, this is just a note to say thanks for looking in on my parents. Also congratulations again on the *Journal* piece.

Our very best to you and Ruthie,

J.T.

From: Jake Smigarowsky
U. of Sask.

7 October 1976

Dear J.T.,

Sorry to fire a note right back at you, but there are a few things I wanted to mention.

Thanks for yours of the 3rd and your welcome comments on my article. Did you really like it? Of course I'd be delighted to lecture to your senior class. Don't know when I'll be able to get to Toronto, though. I wrote that piece, by the way, back before last Christmas. Had to do some revisions in it in response to comments by referees (who took two months), then re-submit and wait another nine months before it finally appeared in print. So I have some idea of what you've been going through recently, bucko.

How do you stand these days on the wage and price controls issue and Labour's upcoming day of protest? This whole thrash is giving me fits in trying to make up my mind. Our pal Ed Broadbent isn't exactly burning up the track, I think. Great guy, but so far as a politician he seems to be a helluva good professor. Still, if I had to choose between him and the available Yankee talent, Ford and Carter, I damned well know whom I'd pick.

Speaking of pals, Spence T. is taking your name in vain around here. I gather you snapped his garters. He never misses a chance to proclaim that you are an ingrate, and a naive twerp into the bargain. Also a turd, I think he said. Yes, that cynical way of manoeuvring for offers and jobs is not entirely unknown in some universities. Less in this one, thank God. Spence appears to have worked up a pretty good head of steam. His ears start to glow and he snorts a lot when he hears your name. One more crack about "Bohunks," and I'll start to take Tapsell's side. Flipping Celt.

But it's about your father. Always a pleasure to drop in on your folks. Your mother makes me laugh a lot, if not always intentionally. She does blither. Your Dad, though, did not seem to me up to snuff or entirely in good shape. Certainly I can't tell what the hip business is about. I know he hasn't had any falls or accidents. But his colour is not very good. Maybe you should ask for some medical reports. I don't mean to alarm you or make a big thing about it, but I've sure seen him looking better than he did last month. You should write to him.

Oh, and Gandy. That worthy ornament of our campus stopped me in the hall yesterday and asked me to send you his regards. He's much too civilized to say so directly, of course, but I gathered from between the lines of his often clipped sentences that he had written to you recently and hoped to hear from you. Do drop him a line too.

Fond regards to you and yours,
Jake

P.S.

Gandy told me a story that you might like. He realizes that some of his colleagues, and most of his students, regard him as an absent-minded old fogey. In fact I think he has one of the most lively and acute minds around here. His own reputation for wool-gathering, though, may have prompted him to retail this yarn. It seems that before our time, way back in the late twenties, there was a particularly absent-minded codger in the philosophy department named P. Yelberton Leddingburt, or some such, a genial old coot much beloved by his students who marvelled at his total inability to deal with the complexities of the real world, bootlaces and doorknobs and the like.

One morning a student encountered P. Yelberton maundering along 25th St. and engaged him in conversation. "You seem in fine fettle this morning, professor," he said. "Yes, oh my yes," came the rejoinder, "got to keep our spirits up in this wicked world, don't we?" "I believe I've often seen you in the Home Bank down the street,

Professor Leddingburt." "Indeed, yes, I'm just on my way there now. Lovely people in the Home Bank, most agreeable. Dealt there for years, you know." "Then you haven't heard the news? The newspaper this morning said that the Home Bank has failed. It's bankrupt." "Dear me. That *is* a pity. I am sorry to hear it. Extremely pleasant chaps in the Home." "But professor, is that all you have to say? I mean, this may be a tragedy for you. A calamity! It's likely that your entire life's savings may have been wiped out." "Not at all, my boy," said Leddingburt, "please don't distress yourself. Actually, I've always had a rather substantial overdraft with the Home."

Thought you might like that.

Smig

To: Francis Z. Springer
Prince Albert
Sask.

8 October 1976

Zinger –

Yahoo! I've done it. Finished. I've whupped it, beaten the buggers. All wrapped up in a neat package, with Innis all sorted out and hog-tied, and Veblen and McLuhan thrown in for good measure. Am I going to celebrate tonight!

Tied a ribbon around the mother and delivered it late this after-noon. Even cancelled a class, something I have never done till today, trotted over to the Press and plunked it down on the desk of a startled editor. Kissed his secretary, goosed some passing old female citizen, and went out and bought a cigar.

It's been a tough scuffle, matey, but I got her done. Cries of "Ho-sanna!," "Eureka!," "Excelsior!," and "Up your kilt, Tapsell!" They laughed when I sat down to play the typewriter, but I showed the bastards. Virtue and justice will triumph. Zinger, I'm going to be an honest-to-God author, the father of a new bouncing baby book. If you raise a glass and shout and "listen for an echo" tonight, by Krist, you'll sure as hell hear the reverberations from Toronto.

More later. I'm off for a blast with Trish and Cutty.

Tenure, here I come!

Ecstatically,

J.T.

From: Mother
Regina, Sask.

9 October 1976

John Dear,

So nice of you to telephone last night. Your father was very pleased too. Why didn't you let us talk to the children? There seemed to be a lot of strange noises in the background. Is it two hours earlier in Toronto than here, or two hours later? I do get it muddled. You didn't sound as coherent as usual last night either. Dad couldn't understand why you were shouting. I hope the phone call didn't cost too much. Things are all so *expensive* nowadays. We are both very pleased about your book. I'm sure it must have taken a good deal of effort. Didn't you write about that same thing, dear, years ago – something to do with your doctor's degree when you got the grand robe and the hood? I think you said you'll be sending us a copy, and I do hope we receive it next month in time for the meeting. I do want to show it to the ladies in my literary circle. I'm so glad you enjoy writing about Ennis, he's always been one of my favourites, particularly his poetry. Did he ever win a Governor General's medal? I hope you do too John. And I hope you'll tell them to give it a nice cover with your picture on it. Blue always looks very effective on a cover to my way of thinking. Your father still likes Zane Grey better than Ennis but I'm sure your book will bring him around. I'm still not entirely easy in my mind about Dad. He says his leg is bothering him. I had to go downtown and get him some new slippers, and Dr. Woodley popped in again this evening to say something about a new prescription and more tests. I'll mail this when I go out to the drug-store. I hope you liked the cookies I sent. I can bring more when we come to visit at Christmas.

Love,

Mother

From: Wilfred B. Twillington, Editor,
Social Sciences Division,
Chiliast University Press

10 October 1976

Dear Professor McLaughlin:

Our Mr. Williams has given me your manuscript for processing. I gather it arrived only the other day by personal hand delivery. Mr. Williams' secretary said she got quite a giggle out of you. She says you embraced her and positively "pranced," and quite brightened her day. We at the Press always find it gratifying when our prospective authors are possessed of enthusiasm. I'm sure I will find it agreeable to get my teeth into Innis again; he always was a leathery old fellow and, if I may mix my metaphors, a tough nut to crack.

Please don't bother to phone again. We like to keep all our editorial affairs and exchanges on paper so as to maintain a clear, permanent record and avoid confusion. Very shortly I shall present my preliminary evaluation to Mr. Williams and then, if he sees fit, we will be in a position to put the manuscript out to qualified assessors. I have no doubt that, as you suggested by telephone today, Professors Easterbrook and Rotstein would be suitably qualified to appraise your work. However, the Press must follow its regular procedures and ensure the anonymity of its assessors. In fact, we do prefer to select referees from other cities whenever possible in order to minimize the possibilities of treading upon sensitive personal relationships.

Be assured that I will devote my most earnest attention to your manuscript. I look forward to a pleasant and fruitful association between us in this scholarly endeavour.

Yours very cordially,

Wilfred B. Twillington
Editor

To: Wilfred B. Twillington, Editor
Social Sciences Division
Chiliast University Press

13 October 1976

Dear Mr. Twillington,

Thanks for your very pretty epistle, which made it halfway across the campus by university mail, an alarming distance of almost four city blocks, in only three days. A spry elderly gentleman who looked to be not more than 104 years of age placed your note directly into my trembling hand a mere ten minutes ago. He gets around very well, doesn't he, for a legless man, doubtless an unfortunate amputee from the Boer War? Please congratulate him for me on how well he handles that skateboard. On the other hand, if he does not make it all the way back to your office by the end of this week, I hope you'll wish him a Merry Christmas from me. Delivery boys have feelings too, you know. Buy the old sport a beer, and tell him not to drag his catheter when next he plans a prolonged three-day assault up the two steps of the Arts Building.

Although almost fifteen minutes have now ticked away since your note arrived, I'm still reeling from its contents. We'll foreswear Mr. Bell's nasty little invention, all right? God forbid that I'd ever appear to want to rush things. But you shall present your preliminary evaluation shortly, shall you? Shall I take you at your word, then, and trust that you shall also let me in on this evaluation in the foreseeable future if you can find a blind and wounded carrier pigeon to wing it those forbidding four blocks across the campus to me?

I admit, to my shame, to being inordinately interested in a bit of hustle and brisk dispatch in this "scholarly endeavour," as you so felicitously put it – are you by any chance related to a twit named Tapsell in Saskatoon? – and I am most overwhelmingly reassured that you will follow only the most meticulous of "regular procedures." Whew! For a while there you had me worried that some impropriety or vulgar irregularity might have been committed if I'd uttered another *syllable* on the telephone. Perish the thought. Still, you do understand, Twillington, that what you have on your desk represents hundreds and hundreds of hours of my hot sweat. It represents my hopes, my career, my prospect of tenure. At the moment my academic status is a pale and delicate flower whose gossamer petals could easily be bruised, nay crushed, by one tiny mis-step of your heavy editorial brogans. Wear soft slippers, I beg you, and tread most lightly (and swiftly!) through the wondrous paths of my tear-stained creation. And don't frig me about, dammit.

Let me remind you that I am not a "prospective author," but an author. You may not have recognized it, dumpling-brain, but what you have in front of you is called a "book." I wrote it. Take a good look at it, because at the speed you work, you may not see another for months. I am an author who has laboured mightily to bring forth this amazing gem of pure and fiery truth. I have deigned to submit it to your tender mercies only because you happen to be the sole academic printers within four blocks of my office, and not because I wanted to be subjected to a big song and dance about who is or is not "prospective." Before I produced this nugget I learned my prospecting the hard way and I bloody well know what I'm doing, or thought I did till I ran into you. As for referees and assessors and all that, Professors Easterbrook and Rotstein inconveniently may live in the wrong city, but if you can find more knowledgeable students of Innis in Labrador or in Bangkok I'd sure like to hear about them.

Whatever you do, Wilfred old sod, I implore you, I beseech you, do not "process" my manuscript. If I wanted it processed, for kristsake, I'd have sent it to a canning factory. Surely you realize that the proper way to approach any manuscript is on your knees, with rapture and awe. Approach it with crude processing tools and I swear I'll come over there and carve off your knackers, if any, with an equally blunt instrument.

So get a wiggle on, and get your ass into gear.

J.T. McLaughlin

To: Professor B.J. Gandy
Department of History
University of Saskatchewan

13 October 1976

Dear Professor Gandy,

It was very good of you to take the trouble to write in September. I appreciate your comments very much. I'm afraid that I'm not very good at taking advice, much as I value it. You may find it amusing that the CBC called me just this morning to ask whether I'd take part in a panel discussion, tomorrow night, on Labour's Day of Protest over wage and price controls. I thought of you and of your remarks relating to show-biz. I also thought of my minuscule bank balance, and said "yes." I enjoyed your story of Leddingburt and the Home Bank, by the way, which Smigarowsky passed along.

I am also grateful for your information about Timmie's background. Everyone who knew her was saddened by her passing. To me, quality of work and "academic standards of excellence" were never abstract criteria. Instead, whenever I have any doubts about a piece of writing, a small but insistent voice in the back of my mind asks: "What would Timmie say about that?" In retrospect it is clear to me that one of the great privileges of being a student in Saskatoon in the fifties was to work in small groups with, and to know, people like yourself and Timmie, as well as Fowke and Britnell and Ken Buckley. In London or in Toronto I never encountered more admirable people. Were you close to Buckley? Although he was less disciplined than the others, I always considered his the most rapier intellect I ever met.

I regret that I did not see Timmie during her final months, but you might like to know the story of our last meeting. I was attending a municipal affairs conference in Saskatoon last spring at the Bessborough Hotel, and because I was tied up in meetings I asked Timmie to meet me for a drink or for tea in the late afternoon. Knowing that her health was delicate and that there might be a problem, I took the bartender aside before her arrival and instructed him in how to make a very special banana daiquiri for her with only a tiny bit of rum. "Certainly, sir," he said, and it was all arranged. The only problem was that Timmie insisted that I join her in the same drink. Predictably, with only a hint of rum in the one glass and a double lacing of rum in the other, the cocktail waitress confused them and gave Timmie the loaded potion. Try as I might, I couldn't get them re-switched. The effect was that Timmie lit up like a pinball machine on tilt. All her circuits began to jangle. Ideas and anecdotes concatenated out of her in a marvellous spurt of high spirits so that she attracted the attention of the entire room, including a jolly drunk at the next table, who, in a burst of bonhomie sent us over another round, this time doubles. The jig was up.

It was very difficult (given Timmie's considerable bulk, tiny feet, and slow mode of locomotion at the best of times) to cajole and manoeuvre her out of the bar toward a cab. At the taxi rank we bumped into the provincial Minister of the Treasury, good old Walter Smishek. Walter tried very hard to introduce us to his companion named Al, while at the same time I, in dismay and confusion, was trying to give the stunned taxi driver two dollar bills to pay Timmie's fare home. But she would have none of it. She kept burbling that the ride should cost only one dollar and repeatedly snatched the money out of the driver's hand and thrust it out of the window at me. All the while Walter kept pulling at my elbow and insisting, "I want you to meet Al." It turned out that Al was the estimable Premier Allan Blakeney, who had some difficulty figuring out what the hell was going on. So my last view of Timmie, which I cherish, was one of her more than somewhat tiddled, twittering away cheerfully, shouting at the driver, and throwing dollar bills out of a taxi as it drove away, leaving an open-mouthed Premier blinking on the sidewalk. She left a lot of us blinking.

And Timmie was a great teacher. She goaded and stretched us all. I'm not sure, Professor Gandy, why you seem so inclined to downplay if not denigrate teaching. As a skilful practitioner of the art, I'd have thought you'd champion it.

Please tell Smig that I finished my manuscript on Innis, Veblen, etc., and that I am rejoicing to have it done. (The day I delivered the whole kaboodle to the Press I cancelled a class – the only time I've done that in three years.) Innis once said that any book on "Canadian economic ideas" might as well be titled *On Snakes in Ireland*; I hope I have demonstrated that he proved himself wrong.

Very best regards,

J.T. McLaughlin

To: Dad
Regina, Sask.

13 October 1976

Dear Dad,

Well I sure am glad to have that book done. I've been working at it pretty steadily. Haven't had much time to write letters; you know how it is. I couldn't

Hi Dad,

The Roughriders sure are doing very well this year. Are you getting to many games? I hear you had some early snow out there and

My dear Father,

Mom tells me that you still have that pain in your hip, and I sure am sorry to hear that. I took the liberty of calling Dr. Woodley the other day, just to be sure that you are getting the very best attention. You know I wouldn't try to give you advice, Dad, or to pry, but Woodley seems uneasy and uncertain as to

> (*Shit. I don't need Twillington to tell me that this isn't going to work. Might as well admit defeat, and phone. And that isn't going to work either. "Hello, Dad? Yeh, it's me.... Uh huh ...Oh no, everything's fine here.... Right.... Of course, Dad.... Yeh.... You bet. That's right.... Look, I just wanted to say that, uh.... You did, eh?.... Good...Fine then, Dad.... Right.... Whatever you say.... Yes, I sure will.*
>
> *Goodnight."*)

From: Francis Z. Springer
Prince Albert, Sask.

15 Oct., '76

J.T.,

Caught you on TV last night, and I must say you have a great face for radio. I hardly recognized you. What's with the beard? How too, too piss-elegantly academic. Next thing I know you'll be wearing Harris tweed with elbow patches or affecting a leather jacket – or perhaps you are more of a suedo-intellectual? That beard is execrable. It looks like the pubic hair of an anaemic mouse. Zing it.

What were you going on about anyway? Something about "corporatism," was it, with passing shots at how big business engages in price-fixing and how our anti-combines legislation is like hunting elephants with a pea-shooter? What else is new? I dug the quote from Galbraith, but you seemed so inflamed by passion or strong drink, flailing about and waving your arms like a whore greeting a troop ship, that I couldn't make much sense of it. Got rather heated, I thought. I do question the wisdom of dumping that pitcher of water over the head of John Crispo, and I respectfully submit that calling the Minister of Whatever an "ignorant twit" and a "carbuncle on the backside of the body politic" may not have been the ideal way to win friends and influence people. Lively, though. Folks might conclude that you are the Farley Mowat of the ivory tower. I do agree that the Day of Protest was a bit of a farce, but I don't see it as anything to get hysterical about. It's all cheval shitteree.

Diefenbaker has the right approach to all this. He merely sits back in the weeds and takes pot-shots at anyone who raises his head, including Joe Clark. It's a joy to see the old brontosaurus still flourishing. Back in August I went main-streeting with Dief. One fine Saturday I tagged along with Dick Whatsizname, the local constituency president, a very good type who has been incredibly loyal and helpful to Dief over the years. We picked up the genial old geezer at the Saskatoon airport and Dick steered him through the out-stretched hands and TV cameras to a car and drove us to Rosthern, a good little town in the constituency. On the way the Chief regaled us with several of his best jokes – most of which even you have heard before, but which never fail to amuse. I break up, not so much at the stories, as at how Mr. D. chortles and hugs himself after he's got off a good one. No one enjoys his wit with more relish than himself. As we drove it was reported to the Man that in one of the towns nearby a new poll-captain named Tessier or Tennier or somesuch had been appointed. Dief turned to me and observed with glee: "Bilingual, I trust. Oh, I *do* hope he's bilingual!" Then he roared with laughter, as only he can roar.

But main-streeting with him is something else. It does not require the usual crew of political flunkies to organize the event and to push people forward. I confess that even a sceptical journalist like me finds it impressive to see the hot lights in the eyes of older people as they press around to shake his hand. I noticed that even youngsters and teenagers, shy at first, kept circling and nudging each other until they fetched up the courage to go over and speak to him and shake a paw. I tell you there's nothing else in this country quite like it as a political spectacle and as a demonstration of profound affection. Politics may be show-biz, and show-biz can create "images," but this sort of thing is not all image. This is a living legend. You can manufacture an image, but you can't counterfeit a legend.

Unlike you effete easterners, we still take our politics seriously in the west. Feelings and personal loyalties run very deep. Apart from the bantam rooster T.C. Douglas, 'r Tommy, no one can stir a west-ern crowd like the old Chief. The venerable buzzard can still rip the flesh of enemies in all parties, including his own. I'd be prepared to believe he greased the football that Stanfield dropped, and he could devour little Joe for breakfast like a Cornflake. Dief has played the King Lear role of the beleaguered martyr so long that he believes it himself, but he wears his self-made crown of thorns tilted jauntily over one ear.

Let's see, where were we? I am glad that you got that book off your chest. My passing acquaintance with the printing trade leads me to doubt whether it will appear between covers till after Christmas, but lots of luck, good on you, and long may your quill quiver.

Here I am living from hand to mouth, without even the consolations of the higher philosophy, gentle domesticity or steady nooky, and there you are gamboling on the verge of tenure and getting ready to hunker your ass down deeper into the academic buttertub. The mind boggles. So you're going to be a permanent poohbah; so you're going to be a "success." Have you really thought about it? I mean, as the hurdler said, eyeing the picket fence, harm can come to a young man that way. A lot of harm. It could be that getting tenure is like joining the ranks of the Sultan's castrati: a steady gig, but irreversible. Seems to me not so much a privilege as a comfy padded cell. Would you ever again have the nerve to get out or to try anything new and different? Will you subside somnambulantly into the depths of the public trough and never be heard from again? I fear for your immortal soul, if any. I shudder to think of you inextricably enmeshed in the coils of cunning Minerva.

I guess it's difficult to be an intellectchool. I guess you know some things that an ordinary working stiff like me doesn't know. Quite possibly it was hard, and worth while, to write a Ph.D thesis on Innis. I suspect, however, that I will always prefer to read Innis himself than to read any book on him, even yours. Sometimes you pampered layabout intellectchools, underworked and overpaid and always bitching, make me sick. Universities seem to me intellectually scrawny but morally fat, like greasy-lipped priests living off the avails of the parishioners. I'd like to see some of you guys hack it in the real world of daily journalism or the marketplace. Half of you would starve to death. And as your Dad would say, if you are so goddam smart, why aren't you rich?

As for me and mine, young John seems happy in his school in Saskatoon writing essays on Oedipus and patricide. Chappie is undoubtedly basking in the ardent attentions of innumerable mashers, while I disconsolately sort through 4-foot piles of dirty socks and rank laundry in a desperate search for something with which to clothe my naked frailties. Occasionally I seek solace in the company of stray females, but I find them unsatisfactory. Young girls are not bad for the snogging, yet they leave something to be desired when it comes to repartee and following the conversation after 2:00 A.M. Still, we must all dip our wicks to keep the faltering flames of fellowship alive.

I think I may take out a little ad in the Personal column of the paper. "Male, slightly used and much abused 41, presentable and educated, fond of gardening, classical music and jerking off, seeks cheerful and mature companion for gardening, etc. Object – clean socks. No triflers, please."

Guess I'll go out and tamper with a polar bear.

Zinger


P.S.

Which reminds me of the departed Betty, and the story told me by the bartender at the Marlborough Hotel.

- What do you get when you cross a donkey with an onion?
- Simple. Sometimes you get nothing at all, but every now and again you get a piece of ass that brings tears to your eyes.

Z.

From: Spencer Tapsell
Dept. of Economics
U. of Sask.

16 October 1976

J.T. Ol' Buddy,

Well, my fine former friend, you *certainly* did yourself proud on television the other night. All we have to do is turn you loose with a Minister of the Crown and a fine economist like Crispo and immediately you think you've got to sound like Groucho Marx, if not Karl. Harpo would have been more like it. You sounded like an addled undergraduate. Can you not appear in public with your seniors and betters without making an *ass* of yourself?

I suppose it was inevitable that you'd have to put your foot in it and get in a lick for "economic nationalism" and other lunacies. I *wish* you'd get it through your head that you can harm your own career pattern that way, and that the economics fraternity does not take kindly to those who pronounce upon matters in which they have no competence. Stick to the pure theory, for God's sake. Bear in mind that in the eyes of the profession there is neo-classical truth on the one hand, and *error* on the other. You, like other nationalist creeps, are in error. I *wish* you wouldn't flaunt your idiocies on prime-time TV. At this point even I couldn't get you taken seriously at Lethbridge or anywhere else. Should I tell the boys that you were drunk? Preaching heresy is not exactly the best way to curry favour with the fathers of the church. I suppose next you'll be declaiming against the virtues of free trade!

Smig informs me that you have actually finished your book and submitted it. At least that's something – now you can buckle down to some *new* work. You didn't mention whether you want me to write a Foreword, but I think that's off till you shape up.

Sincerely,

Spence

From: Wilfred B. Twillington
Chiliast University Press

17 October 1976

Dear Professor McLaughlin,

I have now completed my preliminary evaluation of your manuscript, and handed my report to our Mr. Williams. The typescript, I fear, is riddled with typographical errors and numerous lamentable slips in spelling, as well as some inconsistent usages of abbreviations, viz., % or per cent for percentage, etc., etc. Attached please find on three separate sheets a list of such errors and infelicities. Please correct these on your copy to avoid further difficulty.

In all candour I must confess that I have noted to Mr. Williams some niggles and reservations concerning the readiness of the manuscript for further editorial refinement at this stage. However, having regard to your apparent impatience, I have suggested to Mr. Williams that we might go forward, and submitted to him a list of names from which suitable scholarly assessments might be obtained. I know you will agree with me that the external appraisers should be knowledgeable people from various distant centres of learning whom one might presume not to be acquainted with you personally. Two such assessors may suffice in the first instance.

I really must ask you not to trouble yourself telephoning this office so frequently. Be assured that your manuscript will be dealt with as briskly as possible and with all due care and attention. Meanwhile, please attend to the corrections on your copy which I have of course entered on my copies. We would never be satisfied with a sloppy job, now would we?

Yours sincerely,

Wilfred B. Twillington
Editor

To: Wilfred B. Twillington
Chiliast University Press

20 October 1976

Dear Mr. Twillington,

You did it again. You managed to get a sheaf of papers transported the few steps between our buildings by campus mail in only three days. Those four blocks are really a killer, aren't they?

I perceive that you are afflicted by niggles. Probably you also suffer from piles and other indelicate rectal miseries of the sedentary, not to mention your obvious mental constipation and apparent cretinism. I realize that you are a new boy at the press, only a pale and puerile imitation of a real editor like the legendary Rik Davidson. But get this straight. I want speed. I want hustle. I want delay like I want a kick in the teeth with a frozen boot. I want my manuscript sent to distant appraisers like I want the heartbreak of psoriasis.

You don't seem to comprehend that my career depends upon this publication. Daddy needs tenure, in a hurry, and baby needs new shoes. So roll the dice, kid; damn the niggles, and full speed ahead.

You seem intent upon grading my manuscript like a cattle buyer in a Winnipeg stockyard. I wrung my everlovin' guts out to produce those pages. Writing a book is like having a baby, Wilfred. Let me tell you (may my good wife forgive me) what it's like to give birth. First you take the index finger of your right hand, insert it between your lips, and pull down firmly on the right-hand corner of your mouth. Then you take your left index finger and do the same thing with the left corner of your mouth. Got that? If you pull down hard enough it becomes decidedly uncomfortable, doesn't it? All right, you smart bastard, now PULL IT OVER YOUR HEAD!

I'm sure you get my point, Wilfred. I want you to make haste and not fret about "infelicities."

Get the lead out.

J.T. McLaughlin

To: Spencer Tapsell
Chairman
Department of Economics
University of Sask.

20 October 1976

Dear Spence,

How you do go on, old fart. I'm much less than charmed to find you addressing me as "former friend." Come off it, Spence. It's me you're talking to, the brilliant and lovable J.T., author of the celebrated forthcoming great work on Innis, the same guy who knew you as a pimply freshman, who fought and laughed and slugged it out with you through graduate school. Cut the crap.

No, I do not want you to write a Foreword for my book. My pal Mel Watkins has kindly agreed to do that, and I frankly don't care whether that news topples you off your spindly high horse or not. Nor do I care whether you dangle visions of sugar plums before me, including offers of tenure as Dean of Women at the Aklavik College of Igloo-making and Nose-rubbing.

What I do care about, apart from auld lang syne, is the intellectual divergence between us. It is clear that a major difference arises over "preaching heresy in the church" and similar guff. I do not regard the edifice of economics as a church, nor do I have anything but amused contempt for anyone who attempts to "curry favour" in it. To me, people like Timmie and Harold Innis were giants. Both were, I think, deeply rooted in the Canadian experience and primarily "institutionalists," not the slaves of any rigid theoretical dogma. Both swam against the tide.

So don't hand me a line of bull about neo-classical "truth," and economic nationalism being "error." Fuddle-duddle. Innis was, you'll grant me, a passionate nationalist. True, in the thirties, he scorned the "hysteria" over foreign investment, but he railed against *Time* and *Reader's Digest* as Yankee cultural imperialism. As to your "pure" economics, his friend H. Heaton once observed to Innis: "The American cult of quantities is no mere turning tide. It is a tidal wave, on which Clio's little craft [Clio is the Muse of History, clod] seems likely to be sunk by the swarm of vessels manned by statisticians, econometricians, and macro-economists...." You might ponder the fact that it was not Ken McNaught but Innis, in 1948, who first said Canada had moved "from colony to nation to colony." Christ, Innis could see it thirty years ago and you're still incapable of comprehending it today. You're not too quick, are you, lad?

Yes, I bloody well am against free trade, at least on your terms, dogma and fetish though your ignorant kind tries to make it. With your narrow tunnel vision you can look only south in terms of trading relations. I'd be in favour of free trade with almost all of the world *except* the U.S.A. I think the elegant and persuasive theory of free trade is rooted in the implicit assumption that the trading partners will be equal. The balance just might be tipped if we consider a pygmy bartering with a giant; surely it's a matter of power. But I guess in your terms, "We are all equal here," as the elephant said while dancing among the chickens.

Wise up. This is a new ball game that your American-imported textbook doesn't tell you about. The stakes are high: the name of the game may be national survival.

Regards,

J.T.

To: Francis Z. Springer
Prince Albert

21 October 1976

Dear Zinger,

Damn you anyway for your churlish comments on universities. You seem to think that I've been scrabbling to get tenure for the sake of tenure and, in your terms, virtual retirement. False. I want tenure because it represents the judgement of a tough jury of my peers that I'm good enough to be kept in a university, and therefore good enough to participate over the long haul in the best tradition and the best institution in the decaying western world.

To me, the university is an idea. It is a non-quantitative institution. It is not something primarily concerned with size or productivity, numbers of students, size of buildings, or even salaries. It is primarily concerned with quality. Quite possibly it is the last and only major institution left in our mad world in which what really matters is quality. God knows there are mediocre and bad universities as well as good ones, bad teachers as well as good ones, and soft or bad departments even within good universities. But the pursuit of intellectual excellence goes on in very few places any more, except in the university. It may seem to you rhapsodic or even naively maudlin, but I would seriously argue that in the final analysis universities are all about truth and beauty or they are nothing.

If tenure were abolished tomorrow, I would still want to work in a university. If I were a rich man, I'd cheerfully pay for the privilege of being a professor. I could make, in the past I have made, more money outside of the university than I am ever likely to make within it. That's not why I'm here, and not why I'm so eager to remain here. I would not argue, and you would not believe, that I have what it takes to become a dedicated, single-minded scholar-monk who could forsake earthly pleasures for the exclusive pursuit of truth, nor would you believe that the modern technological multiversity is entirely devoted to beauty, but I'm damned if I can think of any other contemporary institution in which lively possibilities still remain for the pursuit of truth and beauty to be so resolutely encouraged, or even taken seriously. Universities, God knows, have faults, but what institutions do you want to suggest that aim as high, or that still insist on quality? Newspapers, labour unions, churches, the state, television networks? Horse-buns. Until something better comes along, particularly in a cynical age of scepticism and disbelief, I'll continue to hope and believe that universities represent one of the last bastions of decency and dignity in a debased world of lunacy.

Perverted cynic that you are, Zinger, I never thought I'd see you stoop to grubby lines like "if you're so damned smart, why ain't you rich?" What in hell do riches prove, except that you chose rich parents, or know how to lie and cheat and screw the public better than the next fellow? Economists, as you know, are people who know all about money and have none. Asking an economist how to get rich is like asking Jack the Ripper to sell life insurance. Apart from John Maynard Keynes, who devoted most of his life to trying to rescue capitalism from total collapse, about the only economist I ever heard of who was a self-made millionaire was a bachelor professor of some discernment who invested his life savings in the early 1950s in a remarkable technological innovation called Tampax. Every day, when he looked at the financial pages of the newspaper, he'd chortle and say: "Tampax is going up." But I think he learned more from being a bachelor than he did from being an economist.

I am genuinely distressed to hear you go on about "intellect-chools." Truth to tell, you are as much or more of an intellectual than Smig or I. You read and write and think, and live by your wits, without worrying about degrees or certifications. To the genuine intellectual, formal degrees and training are less important than performance and accomplishment. There are idiots with Ph.Ds, as you know, and distinguished intellectuals who were high school dropouts but continued to learn and to produce. Real education does not end with any convocation ceremony. It never ends. Intellectual attainment is rare enough in this crazy world without sensible people like you adopting smart-ass postures of cheap anti-intellectualism, so knock it off. You and I represent a currently endangered species in a materialistic society of Chamber of Commerce Yahooism, and you'd do well to remember who your friends are, and who your enemies. You may not love the Ivory Tower, but what are you going to embrace, the stock market?

And of course it is easy to be an intellectual. No big deal. Given a reasonable IQ and the advantages of leisure, time to read and to reflect, it's dead simple to become an intellectual. Surely it's far harder to be a good friend, a good husband, a good father than it is to be an egghead. The trick is, I think, to be some balanced combination of thinker and doer, student and human being, and not merely an enlarged brain or distended ganglia on the end of a withered or inhumane spinal cord. Being a boor or an animal is easy; being an intellectual is not all that difficult. But being a full person requires a bit of balance and guts.

Then there are the raw, rough worlds of experience beyond the mind and laughable, lovable, sovereign individuals like Mr. Diefenbaker. I liked your account of main-streeting with Dief. He remains an enigma to me. David Hume said that our minds, even the best minds, remain servants of our desires and rationalizers of gut emotions. Doesn't Dief demonstrate that? I think he is one of the great populists, one of the great patriots, and one of the great con-artists of our time. To me The Chief is a good man and a tough man who swam against the prevailing tides of his day and conquered all, against great obstacles, but remained the prisoner of his egomania. He now wallows in sloughs of self-rationalization and self-justification in a way which depreciates his undoubted achievements. Why must he continue to thrash about in an attempt to prove that he was always and invariably right, constantly betrayed, and perpetually misunderstood?

He did it. He can be proud of it. But why must he persist in blaming others for his own imperfections and insisting that he has no faults? I wish he could relax and enjoy his well-deserved position as a national monument. But I think he should now spit less venom and declaim less self-righteousness. Silence is so refined. Self-contained calm would be so unassailable.

By the way, since you are a student of perversity and the limerick, I must mention that the fine biography of James Thurber by Burton Bernstein includes something that was new to me, the backward or reverse limerick. Thurber could create these by the hour, and apparently one of his favourites was:

> A dehoy who was terribly hobble,
> Cast only stones that were cobble,
> And bats that were ding
> From a shot that was sling
> But never hit links that were bobol.

Bet you can't top that.

> And may you never have seals in your bedroom.

> J.T.

From: Jake Smigarowsky
Dept. of Pol. Sci.
University of Sask.

22 October 1976

Dear J.T.,

Gandy has passed along the glad tidings that your ms. is at the Press. Bloody good news, and Ruth and I are delighted; we hope it all comes together for you now.

We've come a long way, bucko. Time does move on. Doesn't seem such a long while ago that we were freshmen together, and now here we are, a couple of rude prairie stubble-jumpers, with our feet fairly well in place on the academic ladder. And you not in Lethbridge, at that.

I can remember when we were undergraduates and I was not only intimidated by boys from the "big" cities, like you and Zinger from Regina, but almost afraid to talk to other students who weren't Bohunks like me. Certainly I was too timid to attempt to date Wasp girls until you gave me a shove and Zinger introduced me to his sister. There was even a time when I seriously looked forward to being twenty-one so that I could change my name to something like Smith, or even Smythe. How the world changes.

Did I ever tell you about my father and the horses? When my family first arrived in Saskatchewan from the old country, barely able to read and write their own language, never mind speak English, and raggedy-assed under their sheepskin coats, they managed to find a homestead north of Prince Albert. Any damned fool could now tell you not to attempt to farm north of P.A., but this was the late 1920s, and any little clearing they found in the bush must have seemed to them like prime land. Anyway, during the first year, the womenfolk pulled the plow. Somehow they managed to get a little crop. With the money from that crop, my father went to Prince Albert and bought two horses. Big horses, part Percheron. On the way back to the farm, father followed the horses, holding the reins, because of course they didn't yet have a wagon or a cart. But on the way home some animal or other startled the team and panicked them. They reared and bolted. They took off. If my father had let go of the reins, he'd have lost those horses. He'd have lost the results of the first year's crop. So he held on. He held on for several miles, and they dragged him. They dragged him till he had a dislocated shoulder, not much skin on one hip, and three busted ribs. But he didn't let go; he didn't lose his horses. Years later, when I was old enough to understand, he told me that the hardest part of the journey home to the log and sod hut was when some children of a neighbouring farm pointed and laughed and shouted at him: "Ignorant Bohunk, he don't even know enough to use a wagon."

He knew enough, all right. He knew how to raise and feed five kids. He knew enough about what it felt like to be called ignorant to send my brother and me to university so that no Smigarowsky would be called ignorant again.

So we all have our reasons to be satisfied with our educations. I guess we all had needs, and all had something to prove.

My father's brother, though, my uncle Nicholas, couldn't stick it on the farm. He went off to the city. Did quite well, too. Fact is, he made his fortune before he learned to speak much English. Got together a considerable pile of money when he knew only three words of English. Those three words were: "Stick 'em up!" My father always wondered whether there wasn't some Eye-talian blood in Nicholas, somehow. There's a bit of back-handed racism in us all. Damned if I know how this unlikely country holds together. But here's an open invitation: if you ever hear me, or my kids, or anyone else for that matter, stoop to telling Newfy jokes or making racist cracks, tell 'em about my father and the horses.

That may explain to you, my friend, some of my hang-ups and why I make a point of visiting your father when I'm in Regina. Which I did again last weekend. J.T., your father is not well. I hope and trust it's a small and temporary ailment, but if you haven't yet been in touch with his doctor, I think you should be, just to be certain. Frankly, although his spirits were good, and he poured me a lot of that fierce homemade hooch, he is not very mobile, can hardly put any weight on one leg, and there is a grey pallor to his skin that I don't much like. Sorry to tell you, but thought I should. Hope I'm wrong. Seeing your book undoubtedly will do him a power of good, but seeing you might be even better.

I'm trying to tell you that Innis was Innis, and Gandy is Gandy, but each of us has only one father. He'd like to hear from you.

Ruth and I send our love,

Smig

To: Dad
Regina, Sask.

26 October 1976

Dear Dad,

I'm very sorry to hear that your leg and hip still pain you. Undoubt-edly it's only one of those passing aches that will be gone in no time. If I know you, you'll soon be on your feet again and up and around.

Meanwhile, it is not too early to think about Christmas. Pressure of work makes it impossible for me to come out to Regina for a visit in the near future. However, both Patricia and I hope that you and Mom will come to Toronto and spend Christmas with us. The kids particularly look forward to seeing you. You are their favourite Grampa. Do book airline tickets early, and plan to spend a couple of weeks here with us.

We all look forward to seeing you.

Regards,

J.T.

P.S.

Tell Mom not to bother bringing any baking. We still have some of the last batch of cookies she sent.

From: Francis Z. Springer
Prince Albert

27 Oct., '76

J.T.,

Barney is giving me fits. As an editor Barney Hockley would make a very good undertaker: everything he writes should go into a little box and be buried. He keeps nagging me to bash out editorials about the constitution and patriation. It all bores the ass off me. Barney is also steamed up about the American presidential election and wants me to write editorials about it. He seems obsessed by Jimmy Carter's interview with *Playboy*. Barney has a salacious mind. Apparently he believes that all girls under 25 fold out in three sections and have staples in their navels. Would 'twere true.

But the U.S. election seems to me almost as boring as the Canadian constitution. The provincial election in Quebec, on the other hand, is more interesting. As a journalist, I read between the lines of wire service reports from Quebec and get the sense of an impending upset. There's a whiff of something new in the air in that election. It almost reminds me of the political climate in Saskatchewan when the social-ists first swept into office in 1944. Was it '44? I have no memory for figures unless they are in a C-cup.

Apart from René Lévesque the only politician who much inter-ests me at the moment is Earl Butz. I was extremely disheartened to see Butz dumped as U.S. Secretary of Agriculture merely for observ-ing that what black folks wanted was "loose shoes, tight pussy, and a warm place to shit." But that's politics for you: a man gets fired for telling the truth. Never mind about the blacks. What Butz said was truthfully what ALL sensible people want, but more than they can expect from governments. If any government could deliver all that, then we'd really have a welfare state. I gave some thought to starting a "Butz for President" movement, but I guess the idea is too late, and too idealistic. Maybe the concept would have more political mileage as a slogan if we cleaned it up a bit, something like, "tight weekends with loose bartenders, tight women in loose dresses (loose women in tight dresses?), and a hot connection to the local pusher." Whatever.

On less serious subjects, I got a good chuckle out of your romantic bleat about truth and beauty and the universities. There's one born every minute, as Barnum used to say, but if that's your story, you stick with it, and bless your credulous little heart. To my way of thinking, most real education is self-education, and for every Professor Gandy you find there are ten Tapsells running the show and making sure that any new idea is modified out of existence by three boards, four committees and a dozen sub-committees. Maybe a genuine idea would still have a chance to surface in a small liberal arts college, but I fear it would be shot down quickly in any large, group-think factory. The problem is size, I think. No large and complex institution seems able to tolerate or cope with real eccentricity, yet only the eccentrics are likely to produce much of value. Bigness is the enemy, like Toronto. But that's another story, as Scheherazade said to the Caliph of Samarkand, thereby keeping her head while all about her were losing theirs and blaming it on Hugh Hefner.

I relished your bit from Thurber, speaking of art forms, and yes, I admit defeat by the backward limerick. Tried it, but the only thing I could come up with on short notice is:

> A sexual whose persuasion was homo
> Made a motion attempting self promo;
> Vertising ads for his rear
> In exchange for free beer
> And ended needing seltzer of bromo.

Obviously it needs a bit of work. What I intend to do is apply for a large Canada Council grant in order to take a year off and polish it up. Isn't that how you academics do it?

However, I have discovered a notable limerick which has the singular merit of containing only one word in its last two lines. Naturally it is a compound German word, and extremely arcane. (This should get their attention at the Canada Council.) Only trouble is, it requires some preamble. It seems there was an enterprising salesman named Bellschaft who made a fortune selling bagpipes in Germany years ago. The Germans call bagpipes "dudelsachs." The trade was so brisk that Bellschaft opened branch offices all over Europe, and even in Constantinople. But he over-extended himself, and when World War I came along the bottom dropped out of dudelsachs sales, even in Turkey. Wandering despondently in a field near Constantinople one day, he decided to end it all by throwing himself down a disused well. Near the scene of his unfortunate demise, his company erected a cairn to his memory with a plaque which bore this inscription:

> An enterprising salesman named Bellschaft
> Threw himself down an Ottoman well-shaft
> And thus did abolish
> Konstantinopolishche-
> Dudelsachspheiffengesellschaft.

Top that one if you can. James Thurber indeed. (I got that from a failed drama critic who says he heard it from Mavor Moore, but I beg leave to doubt it.)

Yours for better dudels,

Zinger

P.S.

Yes, Diefenbaker continues to flourish and to shoot from the hip, bless him. He remains a particularly cherished hero here in Prince Albert. Incidentally, the P.A. constabulary recently charged an acquaintance of mine with possession of pornographic material. Seems they caught him red-handed with a book by Dalton Camp.

Z.

From: Wilfred B. Twillington,
Chiliast University Press

28 October 1976

Dear Professor McLaughlin,

In response to your frequent telephone calls I can say only that we are not yet in receipt of the written appraisals of your manuscript from the two external assessors.

Please rest assured that these appraisals will be forwarded to you as soon as they become available. Frequently it takes as long as two months for busy scholars to read and consider a manuscript, as well as to commit to paper their considered comments. Excessive haste may often be counterproductive.

You will be hearing from me shortly.

Yours faithfully,

Wilfred B. Twillington
Editor

To: Wilfred B. Twillington,
Chiliast University Press

1 November 1976


Dear Twilly,

You sure know how to be slow and evasive, don't you? And even with a short note that says exactly nothing you manage to be ponderous. How does it happen that you didn't go into politics? There, your talents would be appreciated. Meanwhile, I'm sweating vinegar.

But here's a line you can use to torture other poor authors; my young son brought it home from school the other day, and I'm sure that it will appeal to your lively (if juvenile) sense of editorial sadism.

Question: How do you keep a jackass in suspense?

Answer: I'll let you know later.

Get it on, Twilly, for Gawd's sweet sake, get it on.

Yours in agony,

J.T. McLaughlin

From: Francis Z. Springer,
Prince Albert

7 Nov., '76

J.T.,

Your faithful correspondent begs to report that he is living alone again. Recently I hooked up with a very likely prospect named Cynthia, and she moved in for a while. She even attended to the laundry problems (although she made me burn my socks and buy new ones – the neighbours began to complain about strange odours). Many's the glorious musical evening we spent together, lolling around in front of a log fire. I played my Jimmy Rushing and Sidney Bechet records while she blew inspired arpeggios and glissandos on the old skin flute. It's a nice change from the usual percussion instrumentation, not to mention the five fingered exercise as a solo. Turned out that she had very limited conversation, though. I'll grant that she had certain commendable musical and domestic skills, but when in the course of a single evening she asked me "Who is Louis Armstrong?" and "Who is W.O. Mitchell?," I knew she had to go.

My trouble with women is the familiar one; I can't get along with them, and I can't get along without them. And so they come and go. I can't stand being surrounded by imbeciles and illiterates. Bad enough with mental basket cases like Dowie and Barney in the office, but one can't really abide that sort of thing around the house. Chappie has her faults, but at least she is literate and doesn't derail all trains of thought by making puns, or confusing Tom Robbins with Harold Robbins.

By the way, I don't suppose you've heard from Chappie recently? It's a fine howdoyoudo when a wife won't even write to her own husband. But I guess she'll have had enough of the teaching nonsense by the end of the term and will be home for Christmas, don't you think?

On the U.S. presidential, Carter just squeezed it out, and the race in Quebec is looking worse for the Liberals and better for Lévesque every day. I'm really convinced that –

Aw, shit, J.T., when is that bitch coming home? I'm becoming exasperated with all this. It's an indignity, as Sir Winston once said, up with which I will not put. Not much longer. It's a bloody absurdity, not to mention a considerable inconvenience. I may have to take steps. Why don't you write her a long letter and reason with her?

Disconsolately,

Zinger

P.S.

My apparent "no win" situation with the ladies, in which Chappie is being recalcitrant with me, and I can't abide Cynthia, reminds me of a story told me by the bartender in the Marlborough Hotel. He's a Dief supporter, and mixes a good martini, but is a bit of a racist. Anyway, a tourist is walking along a street in Belfast in the evening when suddenly he feels a gun in his ribs, and a voice growls, "Are you a Catholic or a Protestant? Speak up, man, your life depends on it!" "Well," said the tourist, "you can't get me on that one. I'm a foreigner, just a visitor here, and besides, I'm Jewish." "Tough luck, you bastard," came the reply, "you just had the misfortune to meet the only Arab in Belfast."

Terrorism is everywhere, and in the mind, but mainly between the sexes.

Z.

From: Dr. R. Woodley
General Practitioner
Regina, Sask.

8 November 1976

Dear Mr. McLaughlin,

I am sorry not to have been able to be more informative when you phoned my office recently concerning the condition of your father. I am even more sorry to say that the latest news is not at all good.

We had been treating Mr. McLaughlin Sr. for the condition most positively identified by our diagnosis, namely, arthritis of the hip. However, our most recent tests indicate that he may have a carcinoma, possibly cancer of the spine.

It will be necessary to conduct an exploratory operation, and I have arranged to hospitalize him for that purpose next week. Please do not be unduly alarmed. The new diagnosis may be wrong. If it is correct, we may be able to effect a cure by surgery. In my opinion it is not necessary for you to come to Regina at this time. Your arrival might only agitate your father. Let us see what results are produced by further investigation.

I will keep you informed.

Yours sincerely,

R. Woodley, M.D.

From: Professor B.J. Gandy
Department of History
University of Saskatchewan

12 November 1976

My Dear McLaughlin,

I fear that I have neglected our correspondence of late, but I valued your charming letter of last month. We loved some of the same people, you and I, both Timmie and Buckley, and that is a strong enough bond to bridge the gap between our ages and our experience.

Experience is the great teacher, to my way of thinking, if not the only teacher. I perceive from your letter, and from reading several of your publications which I have looked up, that you may have the makings of a good Tory in you. Does that shock you? When I was young, the phrase "intelligent conservative" seemed to me a crashing *non sequitur*, but now I think otherwise. What I'm referring to is a person who has an open and emotional capacity to learn from experience and to value the good, even against what we laughingly call "reason."

As a young man, I could never understand Tories. They seemed to me mainly bloated oafs who wore Union Jack waistcoats and striped trousers, and jabbered incessantly about the Empire. Ambulatory anachronisms wearing watch fobs, the sort of thing that your Massey College now represents. It was obvious to me that they were the most vicious reactionaries. When they talked about "the public interest" and "the public good," I instinctively put my hand over my wallet and gave it a protective pat. They also talked ceaselessly about "honour," "civilization," and other noisome drivel concerning the importance of being a "gentleman." Sort of thing which doesn't translate at all well across the Atlantic, you know. Mostly twaddle anyway.

Having been born in the north of England, I was sent to school in

Scotland before going up to Cambridge. I was subjected to a stern discipline. The motto of my school, Paisley Grammar School, was *"Disce, puer aut abi"* – "learn, boy, or get out." The masters taught on the challenge and response theory. They set the challenges, and God help you if you didn't respond. Corporal punishment and all that. There I learned the rudiments of English and Latin composition, plus some smattering of history. There I learned that "honour" was what you could protect by conniving, and what you could get away with. Falstaff was right. I also learned that civilization was a remarkable and transient phenomenon which, the Orient apart, originated in the Middle East, crept slowly outward to Greece and to Rome, spread gradually through Europe via Padua and Florence and Paris, and even in the eighteenth century to London, until it was stopped dead in its tracks along about Glasgow.

Civilization is a very delicate flower. Probably it flourishes best at the tumultuous intersection between the reasonableness and the higher sense of values of the older culture on the one hand, and the raw energetic barbarism of a more primitive culture on the other. Cross-fertilization, there's the ticket. That is why Scotland produced such geniuses in the eighteenth century, why Budapest produced Teller and Zilard and Polanyi in the early twentieth century, and why New York became so productive in the mid-twentieth. The jab of the primitive is required to inseminate the flabby womb of the old. That is the reason I still hold some hope for Canada, at least west of Windsor. That is why the regrettable Bloomsbury circle never produced much of lasting value. Not sound chaps in Bloomsbury on the whole, not juicy. No balls. Except on some of the ladies, which scarcely counts.

Civilization indeed. It takes fire and guts and adversity to produce real works of lasting value, real works of art. As for gentlemen; don't talk to me about gentlemen. In my experience in the old country, a "gentleman" was typically a worthless and chinless layabout who lived on an unearned income, rejoiced in being only half-educated, and who spent most of his adult days tramping over his farmlands with a gun, slaughtering birds and other innocent fauna by day, abusing the servants at tea, and beguiling the evenings by getting roaring pissed on bad brandy and puking into the fireplace. Such "gentlemen" we can well do without. Phoney lot of ignorant bastards, if you ask me, and a snorting lot of swine into the bargain.

No, my boy, we must not be taken in by all the fatuous rhetoric of the history books. Real life was not that way, as any historian worth his salt can tell you.

Have I said enough to suggest to you that I have no romantic notions of civilization or of gentlemen? Quite possibly.

And yet, there may be something to be said for the values of the old Tory. Traditions matter. Traditions are not faddish, nor vulgar and fleeting. They become traditions because they stand the test of time and human experience, and they work. I grant you that the main tradition of the British, as with their Parliament, is the tradition of constant change. But slow change, gradual change, adapting to broad experience rather than tacking and veering with every passing gust of popular fashion, or agonizing over abstract theory.

I marvel at, and lament, the sight of my innocent freshman class three times per week. For the most part they seem to me dirty great louts of unwashed appearance and rough demeanour, eager and bright-eyed and willing, but stunted by their rural or electronic environments. They tend to be astonishingly mature specimens physically, with hair growing down their chins and up their throats, but inside, inside they are mostly moral and spiritual pygmies; they have the bodies of giants, but their aesthetic and intellectual capacities, their imaginations, are usually the size of a walnut.

Yet we, as university professors, are somehow expected to transform these rude troglodytes into "gentlemen." To me it is not surprising that universities fail. I am in fact surprised that universities fail so magnificently and come so close to succeeding. The battle is always uphill.

Which brings me back, my dear McLaughlin, to where I began: the possibility of producing civilization. What and how are we to teach? Knowing what we know, can we realistically aim, in the face of all existing adversity, at producing gentlemen?

Clearly, the times are against us. Still, we must try. My argument is that we must not be self-deluding about what a gentleman is, or was. Generally, what the world has called "gentlemen" have been idiots and disasters. It's the gutsy oafs who bash about and create art and empires. The immoral ass is sometimes creative. Frequently he tramples upon "gentlemen" and gets things done. Often the wrong things, but he gets them done.

Still, there was a time when the term "gentlemen" stood for something. It wasn't what a man was – that was usually a cruel mockery and a raw disappointment. No, the appellation stood for what a man knew he ought to be. That made all the difference. That is something which Tapsell, for example, will never know, and Smigarowsky knows instinctively. In the long run, it is the "ought" that matters. Paradoxically, as Hume demonstrated, we cannot logically ratiocinate any "ought" from "is," any glimmering moral imperative, out of sordid reality. But if we give up on the "ought," we as teachers abdicate and surrender entirely. Knowing only an indistinct and indefinable sense of quality and the better, we must blindly hurl ourselves from the trapeze of what is, across the top of the circus tent to the waiting hands of the partner called "quality," avoiding when we can the sickening drop into the safety net called mediocrity. If we give up on quality, let standards slip, and neglect exhortations concerning the grand attempt at "the best," we are finished. The trick is to rekindle the desire for something better, for the best, without appearing silly.

Silly is a favourite word of mine. It suggests the pretentious and self-deluding idiocy of many who call themselves "conservatives." It suggests the ridiculous and convoluted wrong-headedness of most North American politics. Many who rejoice in the label of "conservative" are merely right-wing liberals like Goldwater or Bill Davis who champion free markets or *laissez-faire* and try to restrict the actions of government. They would not recognize genuine conservatism, in the older European sense of protecting and conserving the community, if they discovered it in their porridge. As a good Tory, I have loathed most so-called conservatives and admired many Canadian socialists, particularly Coldwell and T.C. Douglas. Any good Tory knows that what we must preserve is not the individual's supposed economic right to exploit the environment and his fellow man, but the collective rights of the group, the community, the nation.

"The national emphasis is a conservative one, in the lower case sense of preserving the continuity of political existence," says Northrop Frye in the Preface to *The Bush Garden*, "and it is typical of the confusions of identity in Canada that the one genuinely conservative Canadian party in the twentieth century, the CCF, expired without recognizing itself to be that."

Paradoxes. I have contradicted myself. That, however, is the nature of the human being and of the true conservative. I scorn the conventional usage of the word "honour," but say we cannot exist without it. I revile the "gentleman," but observe that we must educate more of them. "Civilization" of an effete and precious kind I also find repulsive, but barbarians tend to destroy wantonly rather than selectively, and preserving civility and civilization is essential to what universities are all about. Ultimately the Tory must trust his instincts and intuition.

And he must try to teach. Your insistent questions concerning teaching have thrown me back upon the stark realization that, after a long and happy career as a professor, I have never been at all sure how to teach. I never could convey, in a few direct and declamatory sentences, what "values," and appreciation of quality, and civilization are all about.

Allow me to quote a man who comes as close to it as may be. He argues that the principal purpose of works of art is to induce intense emotional states and elevated states of mind, the keys which will unlock the gates of Paradise. But such an argument will not impress the Philistine unless you can somehow give him a taste for Paradise.

> And how can you give him that? Only, I suppose, by giving him a glimpse of Paradise. And how a glimpse is to be given I am sure I do not know; but I conceive it is what education ought to do. If teachers could somehow make ordinary boys and

girls grasp the quite simple fact that, though the world may seem to offer nothing better than a little money and a great deal of work, any one of them can, if he or she will, have a life of downright, delectable pleasures; if teachers could make them realize that the delights of being alone in a bed-sitting room with an alert, well-trained and well-stocked mind and a book is greater than that of owning yachts and race-horses, and that the thrill of a great picture or a quartet by Mozart is keener (and it is an honest sensualist who says it) than that of the first sip of a glass of champagne; if the teachers could do this, the teachers, I think, would have solved the central problem of humanity.

Do you like that, McLaughlin? Do you get that? The words are by Clive Bell, from a little book titled *Civilization* which used to be available in a Pelican. Couldn't improve much on that. Except that Bell was rather excessively earnest. An art critic chap, you know, and they do tend to plonk. Both life and the arts are a bit more whimsical than that. Choosing the right game to play, that's the thing. *Homo ludens*, don't you think? In essence, life is playful.

Don't be too solemn about your lectures, dear boy. At best, lectures should be merely intervals between intense bouts of reading. If a student is at all serious about acquiring an education, he will read. Nothing can stop him: not excessively large classes, not indifferent lectures, not even librarians. Nothing can stop him.

At this point, however, something must stop me before I burden you beyond endurance. What gives me pause and causes me to break off this somewhat extended disquisition is a pile of unspeakably tiresome sophomore essays. It never ends.

Yours most sincerely,

B.J. Gandy

From: Wilfred B. Twillington,
Chiliast University Press

14 November 1976

Dear Professor McLaughlin,

We have now received reports on your manuscript from two external appraisers. The news, I fear, is mixed.

There seems little doubt that the manuscript ultimately will be publishable. Several rather kind, if not unreservedly laudatory, remarks are included in the assessors' responses, copies of which (with names and signatures deleted) please find attached to this letter.

However, it will be apparent to you that both assessors find the work has weaknesses. Both seem to agree that it is too short. Evidently they see the need, a requirement which I myself perceived, for strengthening the links and broadening the bridges between Innis and McLuhan. In its present form, it is somewhat difficult for the reader to follow the development of the Innisian concepts which McLuhan adopted and adapted. Tracing very precisely the influence of Innis on the later communications theories of McLuhan and his disciples will necessitate an extension of the analysis, possibly inserting an additional chapter, but undoubtedly it will strengthen and improve the manuscript.

To put a fine point on it, more work is needed. I hope you will find it convenient to rework and flesh out this part of the analysis. With that done, perhaps by some early date in the New Year, we may be able to press on toward a firm contract and discussion of a tentative publication date.

Yours sincerely,

Wilfred B. Twillington
Editor

To: Wilfred B. Twillington,
Chiliast University Press

16 November 1976

Twilly, you creep,

I am dismayed, staggered, rocked by your letter of the 14th. I have
read and reread, with mounting horror and disbelief, the extensive
and somewhat fatuous appraisals by those whom you have so coyly
labelled Assessors "A" and "B". Assessor "A" is clearly a nit-picking
imbecile who would not be satisfied with the clarity of the Sermon
on the Mount, and who would want the Ten Commandments
"somewhat elaborated for greater specificity." Good old "B", who
seems barely literate and crashingly insensitive, apparently labours
under some delusion that Innis and McLuhan were bosom buddies,
great old pals and intimates if not roommates, and that McLuhan
merely picked up from Harold's last sentence and continued the un-
broken stream of consciousness. That's crazy.

The truth is that Innis and McLuhan, early in their acquaintance,
ambled down Philosopher's Walk one day and the topic of the Span-
ish Civil War came up. Both agreed that it was a terrible thing. Innis,
always a friend of liberty, naturally sided with the Loyalists. It turned
out that McLuhan, a recent convert to Catholicism, had good things
to say about Franco. Innis could never entirely forgive him for that,
and cooled toward Marshall. Still, McLuhan was always generous in
his praise of Innis, and remained his most perceptive disciple.

But as to me and mine, I admit you've got me over a barrel. If I'd
had the wit to submit my book to another press months ago, I might
be able to slough off your readers' objections and simply publish with
another house more speedily. As it is, "I am in blood stept in so far"
that I don't know whether to shit or steal second.

I guess you've got me by the short and curly. I guess I have no
option but to respond to the ill-informed narking of "A" and "B". I'll

try. I'll honestly try to lengthen and do more, maybe as you say an entire new chapter. This, you realize, will cost me many more late nights at the typewriter, and probably all of the Christmas holidays. But I know when I'm licked. I'll do it. And when it's done, you jerk, I fully intend to ram the enlarged manuscript up your chocolate speedway. Following that, I will (as I threatened on the phone earlier today) throw your scrawny carcass to the floor and, with a firm grip on your esophagus, throttle out of you the identities of these goons "A" and "B". I will then have them dealt with by Mafia hit men who will break their kneecaps and crunch other of their bones, the thickest of which appear to be between their ears.

But more of that later. You'll be hearing from me.

Yours in anger and despair,
devoted to longer books and
attenuated asininities,

J.T. McLaughlin

From: Wilfred B. Twillington
Chiliast University Press

18 November 1976

Dear Professor McLaughlin,

After your somewhat intemperate and garbled remarks on the telephone the other day, I was delighted to receive yours of the 16th and to note that your spirits are high.

From the tone of your jocular note, I take it that you intend to pitch in with a will and press on with the revision of your manuscript. That's the stuff! If you manage to bring to your academic writing the same sprightly wit and imagination that you favour me with in our correspondence, I have no doubt that we can bring this scholarly enterprise to a successful conclusion. You are a great kidder.

Good luck, keep at it, and keep in touch.

Sincerely,

Wilfred B. Twillington
Editor

To: Wilfred B. Twillington,
Chiliast University Press

20 November 1976

Twillington,

Look, gnat brain, just don't write to me any more, all right? No letters, no notes, no memoranda.

I've chained myself to the desk, again, and I will get on with the revisions which your anonymous shit-heads allege to be required. I will crank myself up and make the attempt. But if you, you moronic whiffenpoof, address even one further sentence to me before I have a chance to work out the new section, I will come over to your office, break your thumbs, pull out your manicured fingernails, rumple your coiffure with a broadaxe, and in general be abrupt with you. Do you get the picture? If you survive the awful carnage of my first physical onslaught, I may even say unkind things to you.

I am not in a mood to be trifled with. Just leave me be until the revised manuscript arrives. Otherwise, I will not be held responsible for the messy consequences.

J.T. McLaughlin

From: Mother
Regina, Saskatchewan

21 November 1976

John dear,

Thank you for your phone calls. I know you are concerned. Your father should be home from the hospital next week. The operation went well, apparently. The doctors are saying very positive things, and trying to cheer him up. His spirits seem pretty good. He's now getting radiation treatments, so they couldn't have got it all out. But we're confident the radiation will do some good. It's all so very upsetting. I'm sure I don't know what the doctors are talking about half the time. While Father was still under the anesthetic, one doctor I'd never seen before came out of the operating room and asked me to sign a form authorizing them to try one other thing. I signed it, but I'm not certain that I did right. He said they intended to cut a nerve that would ease the pain in the right leg. For some reason this involved an extra incision in Dad's neck. Maybe I shouldn't have signed it. Anyway, they made the cut, but when Father came out of the anesthetic, the pain in the right leg was still there and he had lost the use of his left arm. That doesn't sound right to me, does it to you? Still, the hospital people are all being very encouraging and they say the radiation will work wonders. The doctors say it may be all right for Father to travel by next month, and he says to tell you that we will definitely be coming for Christmas. We both look forward to seeing you and the children, but I wish your father wasn't so stubborn and set on travelling so soon, and I wish I could calm down about it all. Things don't seem to be going at all the way Dr. Woodley led me to expect. You do think I did the right thing, don't you, John?

Love,

Mother

To: Jake Smigarowsky,
Dept. of Political Science,
University of Saskatchewan

24 November 1976

Smig,

You were trying to tell me, weren't you Smig? You were trying to tell me in your recent letters that things were not all that good. Thank you for the attempt. I was too preoccupied with my own concerns to read between the lines of your letters. And now it seems that the world is crashing down around my ears.

A phone call to the hospital tonight finally got me through to some intern or other who confirmed that Dad has cancer of the spine. I gather that they opened him up, took a look, and decided to close again. Not much hope. They tried to sever a nerve to relieve the pain, but even that went wrong, and now his left arm is useless. The whole damned thing was useless. "Arthritis of the hip," they'd said. Holy leaping Jesus Q. Christ. I remember what Yogi Berra said when he first saw the expansion New York Mets practise: "Doesn't anybody here know how to play this game?" And now the game may be over, before Dad and I even learned the ground-rules. It's not credible, it's not acceptable; it's a goddam outrage! How can the doctors do that? Why didn't they tell me? Are we just supposed to fold our hands and let him die? He never hurt anyone, Smig, and now he is hurting, hurting bad.

Later:

But there's nothing anyone can do, is there?

Meanwhile, back in the groves of academe, silly buggers like me are trying to get published, trying to get tenure. It all seems so squalid. Again, you tried to imply to me, gently and indirectly, that getting a manuscript into print often takes more than a few moments. How right you were. I now have to add a whole section or chapter, showing how McLuhan got the word from Innis, and how Marshall picked up the ball and ran with it. It will take a lot of midnight oil to spell it all out, and probably all of the Christmas holidays. I'm not sure that I give a damn. I'm not sure that it matters a rat's ass. It's hard to buckle down when I'm not sure that I can even bear up.

But if Dad can, I guess I can.

Anyway, thanks.

J.T.

P.S.

Before I put this squib into the mail – and I'm sorry if I lost my head about all this – I must ask you about Gandy. Has our old friend begun to lose his grip? He sent me a most extended and unlikely screed recently. All about gentlemen and civilization. Much of it was vigorous and sensible, but he kept doubling back on himself, reversing his field, and almost ranting. He told me that the Bloomsbury set were mostly fruitcakes, and ended by quoting Clive Bell (known to any student of Keynes as one of the Bloomsbury set) as an authority on teaching. How did I set him off on all that? I recall that I asked his opinion on methods of classroom instruction, and suddenly I receive an enormous packet of pages on "Paradise." What gives? Is he all right? Is any one of us all right?

From: Professor Jake Smigarowsky,
Dept. of Political Science,
University of Saskatchewan

27 November 1976

Dear J.T.,

I regret that I did not keep in touch with your mother during the past weeks, and I'm extremely sorry about your father. What can I say? Don't give up hope, bucko.

Make certain that the Christmas visit of your parents, if your Dad can hack it to Toronto, is a good one. It's none of my business, but shouldn't you take your family to Regina rather than have your father attempt to travel at this stage?

God knows I wish there was something I could do or say. We gulp, and open and close our mouths like goldfish, but only empty bubbles come out. Your Dad is one of the gritty good ones; he's had a good run at it, and he thinks the world of you. The old strains and awkwardness between you, with your separate prides and shells causing long silences, can now be dissolved into frankness and greater intimacy. Even silences would be all right if they are together.

28 Nov.

I couldn't mail this yesterday because I hadn't said anything, yet I couldn't finish it because I had nothing more to say. Not sure I do now. But let me try again.

You ask about Gandy. Our old friend is flourishing. He remains one of the few sane people in these environs. Often he forgets things, and often he appears abstracted and certainly "different," but I regard him as one of the last of the lucid luminaries on this campus. Certainly he is absent-minded. He lives at least partly in another world – but what is so ravingly marvellous about this world? If you ask him what day it is, it's true that he may not know, but if you ask him what the significance was of the Treaty of Utrecht or the Battle of Bannockburn, he'll tell you instantly.

Occasionally I have lunch with him at the faculty club. He does maunder. Often he talks a mile a minute, but just as often he falls silent and appears distracted. There are days when, if I defecated on the table, he'd either not notice, or he'd say something like "isn't the chocolate mousse steamy today?" But on essentials he's shrewd. If he wrote you a long letter, there's probably some meat in it, Bloomsbury notwithstanding.

Now, Zinger on the other hand, appears to have little meat on his bones, or sense in his life or his prose. My sister in Prince Albert has been sending me copies of *The Northern Light*, and after all these years I can easily identify the Francis Z. Springer style. Increasingly, the editorials seem to be written by Zinger. It's a bloody lot of formula nonsense, but sometimes he's at least mildly diverting.

For example, the paper has for years carried an advice to the lovelorn column by an aged party named Mrs. Thornton, "Mrs. Thornton Advises." Usually the old biddy advises on how to irrigate your pet cactus, trim your cuticles, or persuade the Unitarian minister not to quote St. Thomas Aquinas at your Bar Mitzvah. All very harmless. However, I believe Mrs. Thornton was absent or ill for a time recently, because the Zinger style crept into some of her columns, as the following items from the clippings may suggest:

*Dear Mrs. Thornton,*

*I have had a problem about voting for Mr. Diefenbaker. I know he is a grand old man, a stalwart Canadian, and our local favourite son. But when he endorsed Claude Wagner as the Conservative leadership candidate, does that mean that a vote for Mr. Diefenbaker is a vote for French Canadian Catholic separatism and bilingualism? I am very concerned that a vote for the Tories and Mr. Diefenbaker locally might encourage those frogs in Quebec not to speak white. Is multi-culturalism the same as bilingualism? Has our Mr. Diefenbaker become asso-*

ciated with a Papist plot, and are we likely to be obliged to write to our Wheat Pool in French?

Mrs. R.T., Meadow Lake

Dear Mrs. R.T.,

This column cannot presume to tell you how to vote, but rest assured that a vote for Mr. Diefenbaker is not necessarily a vote for Popery or bilingualism. You have only to listen to The Chief speaking French to realize that Louis Riel was well and truly hanged, that Mr. Diefenbaker has little in common with Claude Wagner, Duplessis or Voltaire, and that no bilingual civil servant could ever understand or pay the slightest attention to anything said by Dief in French. Or in English, probably.

The purity of our language will remain inviolate, except as it may be used by many recent high school graduates who appear to speak or write no known language.

Dear Mrs. Thornton,

Recently I took a speed-reading course. I can now read more than ten or fifteen words per minute. One of the things I like to read is pornography. My question is, if I speed-read pornography, will this cause premature ejaculation?

Mr. L.R. (Age 13)

Dear Mr. L.R.,

Yes. Definitely. Recent studies conducted by Professor Schnell-spritzer at Arkansas University confirm the suspicion, long held by serious students of the subject, that speed-reading of pornographic material does indeed cause premature ejaculation. Also pimples. You must try to restrain yourself. Stay off the uppers, and tell your friendly neighbourhood pusher that you want to stick with the downers (the little purple ones). The traditional remedy of cold showers may help, but even better will be a rigorous regime of reading pornography more slowly, moving your index finger at a deliberate pace under each word, and preferably moving your lips as you read. This will have the added advantage of leaving your other hand free to pursue other activities, such as stirring your Ovaltine or biting your fingernails. For a short period (say, six years), you should avoid reading altogether and just look at the pictures.

Zinger's answers are pretty lousy, but he asks some good questions. On the whole, I think he does editorials better. I gather that Zinger was under some pressure to write about the constitution, because for about two weeks there appeared a procession of page six pronouncements concerning the British North America Act, formal amendment of the constitution, and bringing the control of our basic law back home from Britain. "Repatriation" or "patriation" of the constitution resulted in a spate of editorial drivel, mostly pedestrian and unexceptionable, until this item appeared:

> Our recent series of comments on the British North America Act has stressed the importance of giving to Canadians control over their own constitution without recourse to the British Parliament at Westminster. Since the British are demonstrably incapable of governing themselves, we can scarcely expect them to govern us. As Sir John A. Macdonald often said, "A British subject I was born, a British subject I will die – if only those bloody Limeys would clean up their own act."
>
> Civil libertarians, however, will have noted that a gross anomaly, if not a grotesque injustice, exists with regard to constitutional provisions for liquor legislation in Canada, a subject dear to the heart of John A.

Anyone who has tried to buy liquor in one province for shipment to another province realizes that the ten provincial liquor sales agencies will not engage in such trade. Any citizen of Saskatchewan who wishes to purchase wine from Ontario must write to, and attempt to work through, the Saskatchewan Liquor Board and pay their pound of flesh in the form of taxes to that board. Quebec has many French wines on its list, at moderate prices, which are not available in Ontario. It is notorious that the Province of Ontario imposes heavy taxes on foreign wines in order to protect the sales of coloured vinegars available from most Niagara vintners.

The point is that all of this inhibition of interprovincial trade in alcohol and wines is clearly unconstitutional.

Each and every provincial Liquor Board monopoly is an agent in the restraint of trade, particularly interprovincial trade. Each represents a conspiracy hostile to the ordinary consumer. Section 91 of the British North America Act gives to the Dominion, exclusively, the right to levy tariffs. The clear intent and purpose of the B.N.A. was to prevent individual provinces from raising barriers to trade. Sections 121, 122, and 123 of our written constitution prohibit provinces from levying duties on goods available from other provinces. Furthermore, there is an explicit proviso in section 255 of the British North America Act prohibiting provinces from raising tax, customs, excise, or other trade barriers between the several regions or jurisdictions of Canada.

Therefore it is apparent that before Canada's constitution can lawfully be patriated from Britain to this great country, we will have to insist that existing provincial controls of the liquor trade, which represent illegal and immoral barriers in restraint of trade, be declared unconstitutional.

To this end, we propose the creation of a group which may, across the nation, be known as SNARLL: the Society for the Negation of Archaic and Restrictive Liquor Laws. SNARLL will work to inform the general Canadian public that existing pro-

> vincial liquor monopolies are in clear contravention of our constitution.
>
> Let there be a loud and determined cry across the land: Respect the Constitution! Provincial Liquor Boards are illegal and ultra vires. Until steps are taken to remedy this ugly and illegal situation, no elected official, public-spirited person, or Member of any Legislature should appear in public sober or ready to engage in discussion of patriation of the constitution. Let the law prevail! No patriation without cheaper inebriation!

You will note, J.T., that even the fertile imagination of our friend Zinger must have begun to flag and fail under the leaden weight of the constitutional issue. Small wonder, then, that he had trouble coping editorially with the election of a separatist government in Quebec on November 15.

When Lévesque and the Parti Québécois swept into power, editorial writers were no less taken aback than the rest of us. Zinger's response was characteristically confused but jaunty.

> Canada, our country, is now up for grabs. It seems possible that Quebec will separate and destroy Confederation.
>
> It is evident that almost each and every politician, pundit, and editorial writer is at a loss to know how to cope with this stunning situation. Toronto's Globe and Mail, with all the sophisticated, urbane and scholarly expertise on the constitution available to it, devoted a special Front-page box this week to the "discovery" that if a province, such as Quebec, declared its intention to secede, such an intention could be thwarted by the power of Disallowance, the constitutional provision whereby the Federal government in Ottawa can over-rule or disallow the laws passed by any province.
>
> What cunning! What insight! It would seem to the august editors of the Toronto Globe and Mail that if King George the Third wished to terminate the unpleasantness between the Crown and the American Colonies of 1776, all that would have been required was a simple Act of Disallowance. Even

*with an Army at his disposal, George the Third found such a*
*view difficult to enforce.*

*No, the fact is there is no law or constitutional provision*
*which can be invoked in this situation. No one knows what*
*to do. No one knows what to say. There are no laws or agreed*
*constitutional provisions which cover this astonishing turn of*
*events. We suffer from acute political inanition.*

*What happens next? Your editorial board is reminded of a*
*parallel, a parallel perhaps best expressed in terms of the follow-*
*ing popular verse:*

> *A homosexual lad from Khartoum*
> *Took a lesbian up to his room.*
> *As they jumped into bed*
> *She giggled and said,*
> *"Who does what, and with which, and to whom?"*

Somehow I doubt that the solution to Canada's constitutional
problems will be worked out in the editorial pages of *The Northern
Light.* (Don't bother, by the way, looking up Section 255 of the
B.N.A. Act; it's a sheer fabrication. But I for one would be willing to
join SNARLL.)

You will be less than astonished to learn that Zinger was fired the
day after that limerick appeared. Usually he is rehired after a decent
interval of atonement. However, the problem is, Barney was supposed to be writing the editorials. When Hockley was called on the
carpet, he protested that the offending squib was not his. Result: not
only was Zinger fired, but Barney was cashiered too. With both of
them out, Zinger could face a serious interval of unemployment.
Dowie is now writing the editorials himself, a situation which could
lead to the bankruptcy of the paper and the end of free western
journalism as we know it.

And you think you've got problems with Innis?

Best wishes,

Smig

From: Francis Z. Springer
Prince Albert
Sask.

2 Dec., '76

J.T.,

Things have not been working out entirely perfectly for me here in
Prince Albert. Barney Hockley, for reasons far too complex to go into
here, has been fired from *The Northern Light*, and I have felt morally compelled to resign too, on a matter of principle, to reinforce
Barney. I am, alas, unemployed, albeit temporarily. Dowie is trying
to run the show and even to write editorials, mostly on free enterprise and pot-holes in the roads, but it is clear he can't make a go of it
on his own. He writes like a monkey with a not-very-sharp stick.
Sooner or later he'll need Barney again, and Barney will need me.

Meanwhile, old pal, do you think you could lend me a few bucks
to tide me over? Things will get back to normal shortly, but I had a
few Christmas gifts in mind to buy for young John, and even a trinket for Chappie, which will prove difficult to afford in present circumstances. Unemployment insurance is not lavish. Could you
spare me two hundred bucks? Three hundred would be better.

I can just see you grinding your pointy little economist's teeth.
Yes, I admit that I have not always been prudent about money.
Chappie usually looked after all that. Overdraft statements from the
bank keep piling up. Worse still, because Chappie took my car when
she split for Saskatoon, I have been without wheels. You can understand that it is difficult to work the bus schedule into my normal
routine. The fact is, last month I bought a little old Ford, a 1955
two-seater. Bought it from a neighbour kid to use as basic transporta-
tion. It gets me from here to Saskatoon on weekends to see young
John. Not much of a car – small, and a poor thing, but my own.
It cost me $400, which is another reason why I am financially

stretched. But if you could oblige me with a couple of hundred, I will certainly repay you smartly, and if push comes to shove and the situation deteriorates, I can always sell the car.

How about it? Money is the root of all evil, but child support and bartenders must be paid. I'll even offer you a fist-full of lottery tickets as additional security.

Please reply soonest, with an enclosure. Could you possibly reach in deep enough for $300?

Yours in abject poverty,

Zinger

P.S.

In the aftermath of the Quebec election, I've been enormously entertained by the hysteria of the pundits over separation. If Lévesque could take Quebec out, which I don't for a minute believe, the general reaction here in Prince Albert would be 50 per cent "don't care" and 50 per cent "good riddance and bad cess to them," plus the hope that they'd take Pierre along too. Far as I can see, the only people who give much of a damn about Quebec leaving are a tiny handful of media pontificators from Toronto and Ottawa, some rag-tag academics, and some Bay Street blimps who worry about their bonds and coupons. They don't amount to 2 per cent of the population. It's just more of the eastern elite's horse shitteroo. East-west "unity" has always been a Toronto fantasy. If you want to see alienation and separatist passion, forget Quebec and come out to Saskatchewan and Alberta. A better idea than Lévesque's lunacy would be for all nine of the provinces to separate from Ontario, leaving Toronto isolated to enjoy its position as the fat centre of the world with no periphery to milk and bilk.

Anyway, send me a few dollars before they are devalued.

Z.

To: Francis Z. Springer,
Prince Albert, Sask.

6 December 1976

Zinger you donkey,

I'm absolutely delighted to learn that you had the backbone and moral fibre to resign on a matter of "principle" with Barney. I'm certain that you had nothing whatsoever to do with the situation. My cheque for $100 is enclosed. It's all I can spare at the moment. I have a few debts of my own, so don't bother asking for any more. There isn't any more, and there is not likely to be until the royalties come flooding in from my great book on Innis, another chapter of which I am struggling with at present, just to make it a more elegant and complete volume that will be regarded as definitive.

If, while you are unemployed, you drift as far south as Regina, drop in on my Dad. He is very sick, and would enjoy seeing you.

Let me, in passing, point out to you a few financial facts of life. As the pimp said to the secretary, you may be sitting on a gold mine. If your 1955 Ford two-seater, as you call it, is running, unrusted, and a Thunderbird, you are the blithely unknowing but lucky owner of a collector's item worth a minimum of $5,000. Seriously, '55 was the first year that Ford made 'Birds. They are rare and valuable. Before you squander my money, send me a lien on the car, or see whether you can sell it.

In haste,

J.T.

To: Professor B.J. Gandy
University of Saskatchewan

7 December 1976

Dear Professor Gandy,

It was very kind of you to send me such a long and interesting letter. I found it fascinating.

Certainly I will look up Clive Bell's book. Thank you for sending along the quotation on the subject of teaching, a matter which continues to absorb my attention. However, at the moment I'm a bit preoccupied revising a manuscript.

Your views interest me a great deal. When you find time, perhaps you would favour me with a more explicit statement of what a conservative believes. It comes as something of a surprise to me to hear you, or Frye, refer to the old socialist CCF party as "conservative." When I was a high school boy in Regina, I used to play hookey, with Francis Springer, to hear Tommy Douglas speak in the provincial legislature. Tommy was always a hero to me, quick, witty, tough and ten feet tall. I find I cannot get my mind around to regarding him as a conservative.

I hope that you and Mrs. Gandy have a Merry Christmas and a Happy New Year.

Respectfully yours,

J.T. McLaughlin

From: Spencer Tapsell, Chairman,
Department of Economics,
University of Saskatchewan

9 December 1976

J.T. Ol' Buddy,

Just a *quick* note to say let bygones be bygones, and that I might drop by Toronto very soon. Do not bother to arrange appearances for me at the university as a visiting lecturer, because I will be there only two days.

I am going to the meetings of the American Economic Association in Chicago between Christmas and New Year's in order to interview candidates for a job opening here (*not* in your field). With the university picking up my travel expenses, I thought I might as well pop over from Chicago to Toronto. Perhaps we could have dinner together. Will Patricia *insist* on my staying with you? That would be O.K.

I'll phone you from Chicago, and be in Toronto on the evening of the 29.

See you soon,

Spence

To: Spencer Tapsell
Chairman
Dept. of Economics
University of Sask.

12 December 1976

Dear Spence,

There you go again, you blithering idiot. Off to Chicago then, are you, with your colonial tail between your legs to make obeisances to Yankee economic gods and worship at the shrine of Uncle Milty Friedman? If you are not, in the cute current cant of the Marxist slogans, a "running-dog lackey of the American imperialist bosses," why do you bark so loudly and wag your podgy tail so enthusiastically as you scamper south to Chicago?

What a place to go looking for economists! There you are certain to find scholars ignorant of Canadian experience, innocent of Canadian differences from the southern part of North America, and totally predisposed by their training to misunderstand our problems. If you are not looking in Canada for Canadians, and I grant you there may be something narrow and parochial in that, at least advertise in British and other European journals; look in London or Paris or Tokyo or Melbourne for people whose training is not exclusively in American quantitative bunk.

Recently I met a young American Ph.D, extremely bright and personable and open, who was looking for a job here in Toronto. That he had a first-class brain was evident, but our conversation disclosed that he had never read Schumpeter, or Veblen, or Karl Polanyi, and had never even heard of Joan Robinson. I mean, what sort of a tiny, enclosed, bottom-of-the-Grand-Canyon universe are these guys raised in? And Spence, the poor blighter was a nationalist. Really. His (different) nationalism made mine seem pale and frail by comparison. You see, these guys, with the best will in the world, are so nationalistic that it is merely a deep and implicit assumption; they don't even KNOW that they are nationalists, which is the worst type. Because their technology and ideology are sweeping the world,

Viet Nam excepted, and because they assume that's a good thing, these guys actually believe they are *Internationalists* when actually they are blithe Imperialists sent forth from the Mother Country to spread the dubious joys of a unique and particular brand of quantitative American liberal dogma. If you can't perceive that, then you never studied with Gandy the stories of the Roman and British Empires, and bad cess to you.

Here's a little old fat quote for your little old fat head to ponder. "The application of the economic theories of old countries to the problems of new countries results in a new form of exploitation with dangerous consequences. The only escape can come from an intensive study of Canadian economic problems and from the development of a philosophy of economic history suited to Canadian circumstances." That was not said by Abe Rotstein or Mel Watkins in 1976. It was in fact written by a chap named Innis in 1929.

Does it prove anything? Maybe not. But it does remind me of the story of the English explorer crossing the Sahara with an Arab guide. They ran out of water, and when they stumbled to the next oasis they found it dry. The Englishman, parched with thirst, kept licking his lips. The more he licked them, of course, the more cracked and painful they became. Finally, he noticed that his guide was not suffering to the same extent, so he asked, "Do you natives have some secret or technique which enables you better to withstand this dreadful thirst?" "Yes, Effendi, what we do is we approach the rear of the camel like this and, taking the index finger, we thrust it deep into the camel's nether orifice. Then we run the finger around the outer edges of our lips like so." "Good God," gasped the horrified Englishman, "does that really help you deal with thirst?" "No," replied the Arab calmly, "no, it doesn't help much, but it sure makes you stop and think twice before you lick your lips."

By all means do come and visit us in Toronto, Spence, but if you're going to Chicago, stop and think twice before you lick your lips over American goodies.

Regards,

J.T.

From: Francis Z. Springer,
Prince Albert, Sask.

14 Dec., '76

J.T.,

I thank you for your tiny cheque, stingy and inadequate as it is.

If I read you rightly, you seem to be suggesting that the little car I bought in the fall is worth keeping. A collector's item, did you say? But I like it! Surely you are not implying that I could be so crass as to sell a cherished possession for mere lucre. It is a most sprightly car. I wouldn't dream of selling it. It is old, though. Because she occasionally breaks down or fails to start on winter mornings and causes exasperation, I call her Xanthippe. You'll remember that was the name of Socrates' wife, who caused the old philosopher some domestic vexation, a subject with which I am all too familiar. I do acknowledge, though, that your news of her remarkable market value is not without interest to a shabby-genteel journalist in straitened circumstances. Perhaps you'd like to send me another cheque, just to tide me over, now that you know I have such impressive collateral?

Since you seem to know so much about cars, maybe you could find some parts for a vehicle owned by my friend Stiffy. He tells me he has had no luck finding a starter and a rear tail-light to fit his elderly car. He's not even sure how old it is. It has the name "Pungs-Finch" on the radiator. No one locally seems to stock parts for it. Do you think you could mail us some parts from Toronto? Stiffy would appreciate it.

Keep those letters and cheques coming.

Zinger

P.S.

In my excitement concerning cheques and cars, I forgot what I started to write about.

Do you remember the word games we used to play in high school? There were some, as I recall, that we used to ape from our distant and undoubtedly distorted perception of the etymological drolleries played by *The New Yorker* magazine set at the Algonquin Round Table. Does anyone read *The New Yorker* any more?

At any rate: I can give you a sentence using the word "meretricious."

Give up?

Meretricious and a Happy New Year.

Z.

A New Year begins . . .

To: Wilfred B. Twillington,
Chiliast University Press

5 January 1977

Dear Twilly,

I made it. These last few weeks have been somewhat arduous, what with the holiday festivities and visiting relatives and whatnot, but I am sending along with this note the revised, expanded, and completed manuscript.

I hope and expect to hear from you, within the next few days, that you are going to bang it to the printer in short order and have the book out very early in this New Year.

I am tired, Twilly, very tired. Telephone me instantly, the minute you have read the new chapter, and don't feel that you need restrain yourself in saying how good it is. It's very good. It's better than that. Certainly it meets all the objections raised previously by your "A" and "B" mugs. You will see that the new chapter is seventy-eight pages long, plus footnotes. They said expand, and by God I expanded, even though I am now tottering with fatigue.

We're in great shape now, Twilly, right? All systems are "go."

I'll try to catch up on some sleep now, and you pour it on, boy, pour it on.

Yours in fulfilment and completion,

J.T. McLaughlin

To: Francis Z. Springer,
Prince Albert, Sask.

6 January 1977

Dear Zinger,

I am too bone-weary to write much tonight, but I want to thank you
for sending me the swell purple tie for Christmas, and to tell you that
I did not fall for your preposterous line concerning the Pungs-Finch.
Any old-car buff can tell you that there is only ONE known Pungs-
Finch in existence; the odds on your finding one in Prince Albert are
about a half of an eighth of boo-all, and if you think I'm going to bite
on a friend of yours actually possessing one, you've got another think
coming. Who is "Stiffy" anyway? Surely he knows that the legendary Pungs-Finch outfit produced its last car in 1910. Don't try to
con me.

Did you and Chappie get together for Christmas? I hope so, but
the one time I phoned there was no answer at your place.

Here in Toronto, after a prolonged series of phone calls back and
forth from Regina, my parents showed up to spend the holidays with
us. My father got out of hospital in early December, in somewhat
ropey shape, but hanging in. The old boy sure has guts. The remarkable thing is, they did not fly to Toronto. Dad announced in no
uncertain terms that he was coming here to see the kids, and damn
the torpedoes. He then loaded Mom and himself into his big Chrysler
and drove to Toronto. He did not fly, but bloody well drove! Made
the trip in three days, and seemed to think nothing of it.

Lord, how he loves the kids, and how the kids worship him. He
took them shopping, and for walks, and tobogganing and to three
movies. He's lost a lot of weight, and is grey and gaunt, but he's hell
for cheerful. I avoided talking politics with him, and as if by
unspoken treaty, he avoided discussing universities, religion, the
Committee for an Independent Canada, minority groups or French
Canadians with me. This left us with almost precisely zero to talk
about, except the kids. The silences were often long. Then we'd talk

about Jocelyn and Robby some more, after which he'd clam up again, and light his pipe and stare at me in wordless thoughtfulness. After we had stared (or beamed) at each other like a couple of deaf mutes for a decent interval after dinner, Mom would nudge him off to bed and I would return to my study in the basement to bang out another anguished page or two on Innis.

Those two weeks of my parents' visit must have been the longest two weeks of my life. There was so much to say. There was so much to express. Yet most of the real and serious topics, including the prospects of radiation treatments, could not be mentioned. And so, almost nothing was said. I did not, could not, tell him – the things I had in mind to tell him. There were lots of quiet moments. Family silences. After the children were bundled off to bed, we all stared into the fireplace, each searching for the flickering images of our intimately connected but separate realities, and ended by murmuring to each other whether we wanted or did not want another snifter of brandy. "Oh, that's very thoughtful of you. But no, thanks." "Are you sure? Just a touch?" "No, thanks very much." "A candy? A Turtle? Is there any news of your neighbours the Langlys?" "Um. Nothing much new there." "Dad, we should be going off to bed now. You promised the doctors you'd get your rest." "Well. Yes. I suppose so. Tomorrow's another day, isn't it? Another day. Yes." "See you in the morning then." "Goodnight." "Goodnight all." "And I wanted to say that – but I guess it will keep till the morning." "Of course. You bet. See you in the morning." "Goodnight."

And so we live our lives through fitful, ineffable inanities and wonder why other people are not contained and reasonable like us. We smilingly exchange cufflinks and gift-wrapped socks, and marvel at how other folks are not as warm and open and loving as we are, why the human condition is not more simple and tolerable.

Anyway. I hope you did better.

Regards,

J.T.

From: Wilfred B. Twillington,
Chiliast University Press

8 January 1977

Dear Professor McLaughlin,

After looking through the corrections and revisions you have made in the manuscript, plus the new chapter which you have added, I confess that I am not unimpressed. It is clear that you have accomplished a great deal of work in recent weeks. The new chapter certainly is lengthy and discursive.

I have today sent copies of the manuscript, as revised, back to the external appraisers. As soon as their comments have been received, I will be able to let you know where we stand.

Yours faithfully,

Wilfred B. Twillington
Editor

To: Wilfred B. Twillington,
Chiliast University Press

10 January 1977

Twilly,

You crashing great asshole. No, no! Why would you send it back out to readers? I've done everything that they asked me to do, haven't I? I've done it fully and in painful detail. Furthermore, I did it quickly. I worked like stink, all through the Christmas holidays.

You will drive me to an early grave, Twilly. I thought we were done, all wrapped up. And now you tell me that you've sent it out again for additional critical farting and fumbling. Is there to be no end to this? Will you never get off my back?

Just tell your senior editor, Williams, that I did what was demanded, and that now I want the quick and tender attentions of a printer, not a further round of intellectual nit-picking by a bunch of anonymous bozos.

Roll the presses, man! What's happening here? I simply cannot believe all this.

Incredulously,

J.T. McLaughlin

From: Jake Smigarowsky,
Dept. of Political Science,
University of Saskatchewan

11 January 1977

Dear J.T.,

On the twelfth day of Christmas my true love sent to me 220 freshman essays to mark, a curt greeting card from you, and an importun-
ing letter from Zinger asking me to lend him $200. On the whole, I
preferred the greeting card, but I wish you'd sent more news, bucko.
Did your parents arrive O.K., and were you able to put a few more
touches on the Innis book?

Spence Tapsell tells me that he dropped in on you after he hit the
Chicago flesh-markets, but that you seemed strained and distracted.
He says that you gave him lunch at the faculty club, but refused to
have dinner with him or have him to your house. I know he can be a
bore, but what's the story? He seemed pleased that you introduced
him to the chairman of your department, and arranged for him to
meet some of the staff of the Ontario Economic Council, but there's
no doubt he was miffed by being, as he puts it, "abandoned" in his
hotel, left to get back to the airport on his own the next day, and
generally "kept at arms' length." It's not like you to be rude, J.T. Are
things going badly? Is there anything I can do?

Ruthie and I had a good Christmas. Saskatoon is a marvellous
place during the holiday season. Lots of parties and gatherings and
dropping-in. Just before New Year's, we went up to see my sister in
Prince Albert and I had a few drinks with Zinger. He wouldn't talk
about it, but I gather Chappie refused to leave Saskatoon to see him,
and he equally adamantly refused to visit her. I think young John
was somewhat confused by it all, as I am. They're both dug in to
deeply entrenched positions, and each too proud to send out scouting
parties beyond the rigid battle lines, never mind waving flags of even

Yuletide truce. Pity.

In Prince Albert I learned that Zinger has been picking up a few bucks writing free-lance advertising copy for some "jingle" contest or other. After touching me for a hundred bucks, he told me that he had made a few dollars as one of the judges of a Chamber of Commerce essay contest, and had sold a short story to a small literary quarterly.

But contests seem to have captured his imagination. I know for a fact that he hasn't made any real money out of these things, but the whole concept of the contest may have been preying on his mind. At any rate, my brother-in-law tells me that Zinger is the guy behind a flyer or handbill that was circulated in the bars in Prince Albert advertising a special kind of competition. I got a copy. This is how the advertisement read:

### LADIES!

Make your reputation and your fortune!

### ENTER THE LADIES' PRIME PUSSY CONTEST!

On the steps of the City Hall, at Midnight on New Year's Eve, the Prince Albert chapter of the Glee and Perloo Chowder, Marching Band, Voyeurs and Oddfellows Society (Heterosexual Branch, in Association with the I.O.D.E.), will be holding its first Annual Specialty Talent and Pulchritude Competition – Open to all Comers.

Contestants are urged to wear stockings, garters, and gloves (or mittens). Only. If the weather proves inclement, bonfires will be lit, as will most of the judges.

The Ladies' Prime Pussy Contest is a Women's Lib Equal Opportunity event. If you are female and over the age of 18, there are absolutely no barriers to entry, no skill-testing questions to answer.

Has your face been a social handicap? Do you resent the fact that all Miss Teen Canada contestants look alike, as though their interchangeable faces were sprayed with varnish? Do you get angry when these blank little bints announce: "My hobbies are painting my toe-nails and chewing gum?" Then this is the contest for you! It combines fun and a breezy outing with relevant social protest.

An ill-favoured face or even a repulsive kisser need not be an impediment to your climb toward fame and fortune. Masks may be worn by the modest or the bashful.

Win public recognition for the true inner you! Why hide your bush under a bushel? Ask yourself: has your pussy received adequate acclaim and recognition? If you've got it, flaunt it.

Entries will be judged on grooming, resilience, fragrance, flavour, lubricity, plus general demeanour and deportment.

Special prizes awarded for this Sensational LADIES' PRIME PUSSY CONTEST will be supplied by the Multi-cultural Folk-Arts Division of the Canada Council. The judges will be distinguished pussy-fanciers flown in at no end of expense from the Cannes Film Festival, all cunning connoisseurs of quality quiff and quimmerous quattrocento queanly country matters.

No special training or experience necessary.

ENTER YOUR PUSSY TODAY!

Zinger tells me that the announcement of the contest caused some mirth along the local beer-parlour circuit, and briefly became the new-fad party game among pseudo-sophisticates who smoke funny stuff, but was soon forgotten. However, on New Year's Eve at the appointed hour, when he was out walking alone and feeling sorry for himself, he couldn't resist ambling by City Hall to see whether any potential contestants had actually shown up. Apparently the only female person who braved the wintry blasts and appeared on the scene was Mrs. Dowie. She brought her pet cat.

There's a winner.

Regards,

Smig

From: Wilfred B. Twillington,
Chiliast University Press

12 January 1977

Dear Professor McLaughlin,

I do appreciate that you may be somewhat impatient to receive a definitive answer to your inquiries concerning the status of your manuscript.

I can only say that we will be advised and guided by the written reports of the external assessors, and that we will not be able to enter into a formal contract to publish until we have received their reports.

Do you have any other book projects in prospect? Rather than phoning this office each day, your time might be used to better advantage in pressing on with other manuscripts. This one, while under advisement, cannot yet be the subject of absolutely completed arrangements, end-wise.

We will let you know.

Sincerely,

Wilfred B. Twillington
Editor

To: Wilfred B. Twillington
Chiliast University Press

14 January 1977

Dear Twilly,

I guess we will never understand each other. I don't think I can take much more of this.

"Other projects?" "End-wise?" My only other project at the moment is to try to restrain myself from marching over to your office and shoving a sharpened snow-shovel up your keester. If you don't soon give me those idiotic readers' reports and the clear go-ahead sign, I may have you committed for a prefrontal lobotomy. "End-wise," I thought we were all completed weeks ago, but sloth-wise you seem to be a champion. Delay-wise you take the cake. Wise-wise, you seem to persist in being a donkey.

I kid you not, Twilly, your physical well-being and your immortal soul are in some imminent peril from,

Yours truly,

J.T. McLaughlin

From: Francis Z. Springer
Prince Albert, Sask.

16 Jan., '77

J.T.,

Don't think for one moment that I intend to keep up this zig-zag correspondence. It's only that Chappie's temporary absence, plus a brief bout of unemployment, leaves time on my hands.

I'm sorry that no cheque accompanies this note to repay your loan. Things are looking up, but I'm not yet out of the financial woods. Is it $50 I owe you, or $25?

Dowie admitted defeat and rehired Barney Hockley as editor today, so I fully expect that I will be taken back as assistant editor by Barney some time next week. I am already limbering up my inimitable editorial style to do Barney's job for him, and to persuade him to let me promote Stiffy as my special assistant to the Advice to the Lovelorn and other columns that have sagged without my unique talents.

I was most grieved to hear about your difficulties and your father's afflictions. It's not much fun. None of us will get out of this life alive. At the moment, I'm not sure I'll get out of this month alive unless Barney comes through. I'm criminally reduced to beer and Kraft Dinners, and have forgotten what steak or scotch taste like. Why not send another cheque or charitable bundle of old clothes? A mere hundred dollars would do the trick.

You asked about Stiffy. His name is Isidore Gabriel Lafournaise Dumont O'Rourke. He has been a sportswriter, general office roustabout, and printer's devil here on the paper for three years or more. He is a Métis, and claims a direct relationship to the Dumont of Louis Riel fame, but he looks more like a Black Irishman than an Indian, which is probably why Barney hired him in the first place. Because, when drunk, he admits to being an Indian, most of the guys on the paper call him "Chief," but I think that is a somewhat stereo-typed if not vulgar monicker, and since he is a five-foot-five horny little bugger with an enormous dong and a really bad case of satyria-sis, I call him Little Big Horn or Little Stiff-Prick; Stiffy for short. Whatever.

Stiffy has this funny car. It's certainly old, and rather fine, but it lacks a starter and has to be cranked to get it going.

Why do you go on about the Pungs-Finch? Are you pulling my leg about this, and about my '55 Ford too? Stiffy says he admired this Pungs in the barn of a farmer he was working for, ten years ago. The farmer gypped him on his wages when he discovered that Stiffy was a Métis. Told Stiffy that he could have the car, though, if he'd tow it away, which he did. I grant you that the car is elderly and may well be an unusual vehicle, but since it's just an open little pooper with no top, no roof, and not even a windshield, he drives it only in the balmy days of summer. No big deal. All I know is that it says "Pungs-Finch" in brass on the radiator, and if you are too lazy or too fucking grand to help us find parts for it in the east, we'll take our business elsewhere. But ask around, will you? I told Stiffy you are an all-right guy, and I hate to let him down.

Our weather is rotten, and there seems to be a particularly cold front moving this way from Saskatoon. My wife is being chilly. As a police friend of mine says, the problem is not the outlaws but the in-laws. Chappie's relatives have said nasty things to her about yours truly and are trying to poison her mind against me. Chappie herself did not deign to come to Prince Albert for Christmas. She didn't show up here, even once, during the entire holiday season. John came up by bus for one day, but even he didn't want to stay over-night. I'm beginning to think this situation may be serious. Pre-sumably my dear wife wants me to come crawling to her on my knees, wailing that it's all my fault, and begging her to reconsider.

And you know what? I just might.

Best wishes; long may your pung finch.

Zinger

P.S.

I really am sorry about your Dad. If I had the price of some gasoline, I'd drive down to Regina to see him. I don't suppose you could spare me a few more coins, just till Barney gets his shit together?

Z.

To: Jake Smigarowsky
Dept. of Political Science
University of Sask.

19 January 1977

Dear Smig,

Thanks for your letter and your news. I always was a sucker for contests, and Zinger's sounds very worth while. At a cocktail party here recently I tried to introduce the idea as a new parlour game, but Patricia clouted me with a rather heavy marble ashtray before I could convey all the niceties and nuances of the concept. It seems unlikely to find wide acceptance among these staid easterners.

Please explain to Tapsell that I was trying to be friendly, but had other things on my mind. As you know, my parents were here for two weeks, and Dad is definitely no better. He's in considerable pain, and popping Demerol every night. I didn't want to talk about it at all, to anyone, never mind Tapsell. Further, I was working every night on the Innis rewrite, and I wasn't too keen to go into all that, either. I wrote one entirely new, long chapter. Can you believe that they've sent the whole bundle out to assessors again? Here I am with a dying father, pissing my own life down my pant-leg, revising Innis for the 13th time, and bloody Tapsell wants to be a dinner guest.

I'm simply too tired to write to him, or to write any more tonight. But try to explain the circumstances to him, will you?

Very best,

J.T.

P.S.

Re the Ladies' Prime Pussy Contest: does that mean that Mrs. Dowie was declared the winner? It would have made a good photograph for the paper.

J.T.

From: Francis Z. Springer,
Prince Albert, Sask.

21 Jan., '77

J.T.,

Barney is finking out. He is so glad to get his job back that he's even trying to write a few editorials by himself, and he is so uptight about Dowie's wrath or being fired again that he has not re-hired me – yet. He will. He must. I'm down to my last few rounds of bologna. I'm hanging in, but I'm sure not gaining any weight. I spend my afternoons lurking about the pool hall, hoping someone will treat me to a chocolate bar.

But the real news is that Chappie has gone beyond the bounds of propriety and over the brink. I got a ride with a friend down to Saskatoon the other day and I dropped in at the school where Chappie is teaching. You teachers sure have it easy. She wasn't there – it was just after four on a Friday – but on her classroom door was this name: *Ms.* Margot Chapman. By God, I will not stand for such an indignity! I yield to no man in my support for liberal causes, including Indian land claims, Gay Rights and Women's Liberation, but when such causes begin to impinge on the sanctity of the home and a man's personal life, we must put a stop to them. As the Oxford Debating Union once put it, "Resolved: that a line must be drawn somewhere."

I don't so much mind her leaving me (for a time). I don't much fuss if she takes young John and my car, or even when she takes a job. But when she changes her name and affects the horrid Ms., knowing damned well she's a Mrs., that is the supreme disloyalty, the ultimate insult. Treason, it is. This means war. I'm more than somewhat angry now, and intend to take steps. We'll see about this. Let the very gods tremble at the wrath of a Springer scorned.

Zinger

From: Margot Chapman Springer
Saskatoon, Sask.

26 January 1977

J.T. old dear,

Thank you for your Christmas card and your newsy note, as well as your gift to John. He loves model airplanes, and has never had one with a real gasoline engine before. I asked him to write you a thank-you note, but you know how boys are.

Speaking of boys, I wonder whether you could have a word with my former husband? He has ignored or returned unopened all communications from my lawyer for months, but now he is being even more difficult. I know it's a strain on him to be unemployed so long, but it serves the bastard right, and I now wonder whether something may have snapped in the thin rubber band that churns his tiny mind?

Since about last November he has been phoning me and accusing me of entertaining "young Lotharios." He really seems to believe that I am being courted and pursued by rows and rows of swinging young stockbrokers (if you know of a *single* one, will you give him my address?), and that I am "putting out," as he so charmingly puts it, for everyone from my Principal to my grade-nine boys. If I'm not at home when he calls, he assumes that I am working the late shift at some bordello. I don't know how or why he tries to keep track of me from that distance, but I wish he could distinguish between a PTA meeting and a weekend in Vegas with Robert Redford.

He has been hassling me. Lately the campaign of harassment has been stepped up to full tilt and flat out. I can't tell you what I've been going through. Often he phones me at 9:00 P.M. to see if I am at home. That's O.K., I guess, but now he follows up the 9:00 P.M. call with another phone inquiry at 2:00 A.M., to see whether I'm *still* in, or to ask whether I was expecting an obscene caller. This week he mailed me a box with a florist's label on it saying "Orchid," but it ticked, even though all it contained was an alarm clock and some wires, plus two fire-crackers and a Girl Guides' cookie. He phoned my landlord to say that I was a dope-user and a hooker on the side, and should be evicted.

That's not all. I've just learned from the Post Office that he has had my mail rerouted, including my pay-cheques, to him in Prince Albert. Zinger has put my name on mailing lists for special lingerie and contraceptive catalogues, and for mail order courses in T.V. repair as well as free samples of ointments guaranteed to shrink hemorrhoids. His most recent letter to my school principal accuses me of being a Communist, a lesbian, a runner for a numbers game, an illegal immigrant, and a supporter of Social Credit. Yesterday he had delivered to my classroom, Special Delivery, a very dead duck, an honest-to-God feathered, deceased, decomposing, and quite dismayingly putrid, dead Mallard duck. Maybe it's his way of being romantic, but I don't much appreciate it. Doesn't he know how to send flowers, for Pete's sake?

I'm not sure how much more of this I can put up with. He won't listen to reason, but he might listen to you – that didn't come out just right, but you know what I mean. Could you, would you, please, tell him to back off? I'm finding this teaching dodge, and all the marking and counselling and interviewing of parents, quite hard enough without being bugged and threatened and assaulted by Zinger every time I turn around. Even young John is becoming a bit jumpy. Francis Z. has not sent me a child support payment since November, but I wouldn't complain so much about that if only he'd stop this warped and mindless program of systematic persecution.

He won't listen to me. He won't reply to my lawyer. Do you think you could get through his thick and demented skull that he is not doing himself any good? Please try for me, J.T. I'm desperate, or I wouldn't ask you.

Fond regards,

Chappie

To: Francis Z. Springer
Prince Albert, Sask.

29 January 1977

Dear Zinger,

Don't do it. Really, it's the wrong thing, and it won't work. You told me that you were angry about the *Ms.*, or some other half-real or imaginary slight, and that you were going to wage war. But don't.

Chappie has written to me in some distress that you are going out of your way to bug and bedevil her. I know how you feel, and why you want to. But stop. Far from being amused, she is only antagonized. If you want her back, Zinger, and I know you do, for Kristsake back off and leave her in peace. Use sweet words instead of crude jests, and keep the door open instead of sending idiot notes to her school. That will only slam off any possible flow of her feelings.

I'm too far behind in marking essays and some other work to write a long and chatty letter or explanation at the moment, but I enclose a new book I think you'll like by Mel Watkins on the Dene People, and I beg you to cool it and give Chappie some more breathing space. Send her perfume, or poems, but don't send her trouble and threats.

In good will and great haste,

J.T.

From: Francis Z. Springer
Prince Albert, Sask.

1 Feb., '77

J.T.,

Thanks for the book, which looks very interesting. I'll read it next weekend. Damned if I know why you send expensive books when you could be sending more welcome cheques or legal tender. I'm still without employment. I'm still on my uppers and broke, but you send me uplifting political tracts and fatuous advice instead of the good old long green. What sort of a friend are you, anyway? Chappie is all right. She's employed and secure and preening under the blandishments of untold numbers of randy young admirers, frolicking about in the sordid flesh-pots of Saskatoon while I languish on the breadline in this frozen outpost of anguish, injustice, and journalistic impurity.

How is your work going? How is your Dad? Do send me news, and glad tidings, but do not trouble me with advice to the lovelorn; I used to write that sort of pap myself for a living, and now I am just barely getting by. Advice, I don't need. Unless you have something constructive or cheerful to say, don't bother me, and don't burden the postman.

Your earnest strictures on domestic pacifism amuse me, but you do not seem to comprehend that in an all-out war, you cannot pull punches. This is a no-holds-barred battle to the death.

Your solemn naiveté reminds me of the story of the Blitz of London in World War II when a Bobby was trying to herd people urgently into the bomb shelters during a fire-bomb raid. An old lady detached herself from the mob belting into the Underground and started to scruffle about on her hands and knees on the pavement. The cop tried to move her along, but she objected that an errant elbow in the crowd had knocked out her false teeth. "Come along, then, Mum," said the cop, "that's not important. 'Itler isn't dropping ruddy sandwiches, you know."

Keep clear, lad. It's going to get worse before it gets better.

Toodle-ooh,

Zinger

P.S.

I keep wondering whether living in Toronto hasn't softened your brain. You should flee from that benighted urban bog. To me, Toronto is the sort of cold, life-denying place where servile people obediently plod in and out of steel and glass bank towers, and when someone treads on their toes in the subway, the owner of the toes says, "sorry." And the owners of the bank towers chortle as they rake in the dividends from all across the country, delighted with the numb national obeisance to Hogtown's gods of vulgar size and Mammon. No class, no style, no reality; just greed.

Quebec, on the other hand, increasingly seems to me an amusing place to live. By God, those Frenchies are insouciant. Where else would you find the Premier of a province driving home no more sober than he ought to be at 4:00 A.M., running over a body in the street, and the cops give the *body* a breathalyzer test? Now that's the sort of place where I could live.

Ho! Canada. We stand on guard for whee.

Z.

From: Margot Chapman Springer,
Saskatoon, Sask.

3 February 1977

J.T. old dear,

Didn't you write to my dippy husband? Didn't you convey to him my message? I thought I could count on you. It's all too much.

Last night, at midnight, at least an hour after I had fallen into bed, a Salvation Army Brass band showed up at my door, standing in a cheerful row in the corridor of my apartment building, playing "Onward Christian Soldiers" and – I can't stand it – "Abide With Me," on their horns and tambourines. My landlord is threatening to have me evicted. They swore that they were hired, by a special donation of a Mr. F.Z. Springer (paid by cheque, undoubtedly rubber), to play for a wake of a Christian brother.

Do you see what I mean? He's crazy. He's relentless. You've GOT to do something to make him stop. I can't take much more of this. Should I call the cops and have him locked up, or what??

Help!

Chappie

From: Francis Z. Springer,
Prince Albert, Sask.

6 Feb., '77

J.T.,

I know you have been under some pressure recently, and I know that you mean well, but this shuttlecock correspondence becomes wearisome, and your loud and addled phone call tonight led me to believe that you're losing your grip.

What can you, what can anyone, possibly have against the Salvation Army? Very decent folks, and fine Christian people altogether. I may, in my increasingly acute financial plight, have to throw myself on the tender mercies of their hostel at any moment, and here you are ranting on the telephone and bad-mouthing them for commendable acts of charity. No wonder you do not have tenure. You seem to get everything all wrong.

Leave it, buddy; drop it. There's a good boy. Old Francis Z. knows what he is doing, even if you seem incapable of comprehending the most elementary of home truths. I don't know what you were talking about on the telephone, but you were decidedly intemperate, and I think you may need a rest. I know nothing about any late night musical presentations in Saskatoon, but even if I did, I fail to see why you should become hysterical about a nocturnal serenade. What ails you?

Yours in Christ, our salvation,

Zinger

P.S.

Did I mention that I have a pet ostrich? Won him during the recent

Yuletide festivities in a game of five card stud. A most pleasant companion, and very useful around the house, particularly in hastening the departure of unwanted guests or, if they insist on staying, as a general ice-breaker and conversation-piece. I call him Mackenzie. With his astonishing neck, he has an endearing ability to inspect his own anus, if not stick his beak up his own ass, rather like a number of politicians and professors of my acquaintance.

Mackenzie doesn't eat much. He is loyal and cheerful. His conversation is limited to certain simple noises such as "gook, gook," much like most American GI's in Asia. He does, inconveniently, shit on the rug from time to time, but so do some of my best friends, and nobody's perfect. I'm hoping to cross-breed him with a buffalo to produce a Buffalstrich or an Ostralo but, if I were successful, he might go into politics as a Progressive-Conservative, a Conservative-Progressive, or even a goony-bird like Otto Lang who lacks wings of his own but still insists on flying.

Z.

From: Jake Smigarowsky,
Dept. of Political Science,
University of Sask.

7 February 1977

Dear J.T.,

I managed to get down to Regina for a day last week; Ruthie wanted to attend some Consumers' Association meetings. We dropped in on your parents, and they seemed in pretty fair shape, much cheered by their visit to you in Toronto, bucko. Your father showed us a couple of gross of snapshots of the kids. It's clear that he is in some discomfort, but the old buzzard hangs in tolerably well. The tapes you sent of the kids telling him their news and singing their school songs are a big hit with him. I know it cheers him when you phone.

Gandy has been offered a Conservative nomination to contest a provincial by-election, but he turned it down. He says no true conservative would want to defeat the Blakeney NDP government, which is trying to keep cable T.V. out of private hands and in the public sector. Never knew Gandy had any socialist sympathies, but wonders never cease, and the NDP these days needs all the friends it can get.

Zinger is at it again. He's giving Chappie rather a hard time. Seems he showed up at her apartment last weekend and, just as he was pulling up in his car, he saw a man get out of another car and ring her buzzer. Without further ado Z. marched back to the intruder's vehicle, took a rock from the edge of the driveway and, amid shouts of "masher" and "rape-artist" as well as "home-wrecker," bashed in the windshield of the man's new Plymouth. Turned out to be the Principal of Chappie's school, delivering some documents and mark sheets. He may sue.

Doesn't seem that Zinger is being cool.

Regards,

Smig

To: Francis Z. Springer,
Prince Albert, Sask.

10 February 1977

Zinger,

Why will you not leave that woman alone? What do you think you are accomplishing by destroying cars and smashing in windshields? Chappie is becoming distraught, terribly on edge, which is a bloody bad thing to inflict on anybody. It is juvenile and counterproductive; it will do you absolutely no good at all. You are being an ass.

And why are you trying to con me with all these improbable tales? I no more believe that you have an ostrich than that Stiffy, if he exists, is the owner of a Pungs-Finch. Presently I am plagued by some of my own preoccupations. My lectures are not going well, I'm having trouble settling down to some new writing for a textbook with Cutty, and I'm behind with essay marking. Could you lay off for a while with the nasty numbskull nonsense?

We both have hit a rocky patch, right? I'm gnashing my teeth about tenure, and you're experiencing job problems as well as tension with Chappie. But do NOT harass her. If you keep on playing Bluebeard, demolishing cars and sending her dead ducks, you may force me to choose up sides in your domestic civil war and, in trying to give your long-suffering wife some moral support, I may come out there and bash you on the beezer with a fence post. For gawd's sake, cut it out.

J.T.

From: Francis Z. Springer,
Prince Albert, Sask.

14 Feb., '77

J.T.,

Golly-gosh and shitty-pies, professor, I tremble before your righteous wrath. A fence post, yet. Threats of physical violence!

Fie, fawk, and tiddley-poo. You are about as violent as two wet noodles and a baby parsnip, and you know it. Don't go giving me advice about how to handle the female of the species. Send me some parts for Stiffy's car, send me more books, send me instructions and kits for macramé or crocheting, but do not presume to send me advice. Ixnay on the shitteroo.

I am O.K.; Chappie is O.K.; you are so-so and able to tie up your own shoelaces. Barney has got me back on staff as assistant editor, debts may yet be paid off, and my god how the money flows in. I even have a new girlfriend, name of Naomi, who can cook soufflés and corned beef and cabbage. What more could a man ask? Naomi thinks I'm the greatest journalist since H.L. Mencken. Quite possibly she's right. Dowie does not entirely share her opinion, but what does he know?

Things could be worse. I am thinking of sending Chappie a token of my esteem. What do you think she'd like best, a singing telegram, a bag of jelly beans, a new canoe paddle, or a subscription to *Playgirl*? A stuffed moose head might be nice. I will give it more thought. Surely you see that I have all the right instincts?

Take it easy.

Zinger

From: Francis Z. Springer,
Prince Albert, Sask.

17 Feb., '77

J.T.,

It's good to have my job back, but I am not writing this from the office, or even from my roll-top desk at home. I'm writing from jail.

Shades of Oscar Wilde. (No, no, nothing like THAT.) We have a very nice jail here in Prince Albert, as jails go; some, I'm assured, are much cozier than others. I'm not much partial to them, myself, but if you must be in a jail, I can recommend this one quite highly. One can find here a considerable amount of leisure for writing.

So you doubt that I have an ostrich named Mackenzie, do you? You dumb turnip, not only do I have an ostrich, but also a lump on my noggin and criminal charges pending. You see, it wasn't Dowie that put me behind bars, or even Chappie, though she does appear increasingly threatening, for reasons I can't fathom. It was Mackenzie who landed me here, plus an elderly nature-lover, assisted by a somewhat irritable constable. Happened this way:

Mackenzie and I were out for an evening stroll, he docile at the end of his leash, and I frantic at the end of my tether after a bad day with Barney. Apart from the fact that a perambulating ostrich sometimes receives startled glances from passing citizens and excites consternation among the canine population, all was calm and serene until suddenly I found myself set upon from behind and belaboured about the head and ears by an unusually fierce little old lady. Viciously attacked, by God, by a small geriatric female. With the gallantry characteristic of his species, Mackenzie tried to defend me, but even he was taken aback by the violence of the unprovoked assault, and he succeeded only in tangling my feet in the leash. Without that impediment I might have been able to ward off my assailant but, ignominiously, I was felled by a handbag wielded by an enraged grandmother, smashed to the ground by a clout between the eyes delivered by an elderly doll whose sizable purse must have been freighted with lead pipe. (Having seen the contents of her purse later, in the squad car, I have reason to believe that the blue-haired little scamp had spent the evening looting junkyards.)

Little old ladies, once aroused to anger, are definitely to be avoided. In fact I am now in a position to recommend that, should the occasion arise, you might do better to face a pair of professional muggers or a herd of stampeding rogue elephants than your common-garden octogenarian female with her dander up.

As best I recall, her war cry was, "Death to the despoilers of the whooping crane!" Do you have anything against the whooper, J.T.? Certainly I do not. So you may appreciate my confusion when I regained my senses and found myself stretched out in the back seat of a police cruiser with this hysterical old party babbling away to a large cop about ornithology, conservation, rapists of the ecology, and the whooping crane as an endangered species. Evidently Mackenzie had been the victim of mistaken identity.

Mac patiently followed the police car to the station where the cop and a burly desk sergeant tried vainly to sort things out. "Sergeant, this man has a whooping crane held captive." "Sergeant, I can explain everything." "Quiet, you. Madam, where is this crane?" "Right outside the window. Look, you can see the rope around his neck. A captive." "Well, Madam, the alleged crane seems to be standing there quietly enough." "It's not an alleged crane, I tell you, it's a whooping crane. I've been a bird-watcher all my life, and that's a whooper. I want this man locked up." "Well, through the window, Madam, it's a bit hard for me to verify that he's a crane. Bob, bring the bird in. Now, you Sir, do you admit that your feathered, er, companion is a whooper?" "Of course not, Sergeant. His name is Mackenzie. Obviously he is no kind of a crane. Ah, here he is. What does he look like to you?" "Not much of an expert on birds, myself. *Could* be an ostrich, but that doesn't seem probable." "I tell you, Sergeant, it's a whooper." "Madam, is there anything else he might be? Bob, what do you think it is?"

Constable Bob, apparently, was not lured away from nuclear physics, but he did have a glimmer of wit: "Maybe a pale northern flamingo?," he offered, scratching his head, "or how 'bout a pelican with a weak chin?" "Good thinking, officer," I put in when I should have known better, "you're on the right track. What do you think about him now that you've seen him in the light?" "Whooper," insisted the surly little broad, winding up her handbag again, menacingly. "Might be an overgrown chicken with an Adam's apple problem," Bob mused. (I was beginning to like him.) "Aha," I cried, "that's using your head, officer. Maybe the lady thinks he's a giant canary with a goiter?" "Whooper," she persisted, but with less conviction.

At this point the Sergeant was decidedly puzzled and a bit exasperated. He got up from his desk and approached Mackenzie, muttering, and apparently wanted to inspect him. Now, your average ostrich is somewhat touchy and easily frightened. Ostriches, when scared, tend to do one of two things: either they run, astonishingly fast, which Mac couldn't do in a small room, or else they kick. They have very powerful legs, and are strong and fancy kickers. I'm sorry to report that, as the Sergeant drew closer, Mackenzie turned and fetched him a good one right in the gonads. Drumsticked the big bugger of a cop right across the room and ricocheted him off the wall like a three-cushion billiard shot. It was a memorable spectacle. You don't often get to see a large Sergeant take off like that. He'd probably still be in orbit if it hadn't been for the damned wall he got plastered against.

By the time the Sergeant came to and regained his senses he had also lost his cool. Constable Bob managed to compose himself and wipe the tears from his eyes, but I was still laughing helplessly when the Sergeant rolled over. Therefore, I became the innocent victim of his wrath. That is why I am languishing in the slammer, charged with assaulting a policeman with a deadly ostrich and various other ornithological and criminal offences. The little old lady disappeared into the night, but the Sergeant is searching the statute books to find cause as to whether he can have me drawn and quartered. If you wish, you may send along a cheque to the F.Z. Springer Conservation, Benevolent, and Legal Aid Fund.

Do you still doubt whether your old pal has an ostrich? There are times when I wished I didn't, and this is one of them.

Yours incarceratedly,

Zinger

From: Jake Smigarowsky
Department of Political Science
University of Sask.

21 February 1977

Dear J.T.,

Recently the Prince Albert *Northern Light* has been carrying spirited editorials on the shortcomings and iniquities of our penal system. I gather that Zinger has a new cause, and is writing about jails from a special and inside vantage point. The story I get from P.A. is something about a bird, and that he unleashed a pterodactyl or a brace of buzzards (versions of the story differ) into a meeting of the town council. One informant gave my sister to believe that Zinger loosed a cage full of vultures and/or crazed man-eating storks among the aldermen in the council chambers. Somehow I beg leave to doubt it, bucko. Seems to me more likely that Francis Z. dropped a bucket of Colonel Sanders' southern fried chicken into a meeting of the Storm Sewer and Parking Lot Committee, but I haven't got it all straight, and I judge not in order that I be not judged. I do know that he is out on bail. Some sort of a criminal charge is pending, and good luck to him.

Closer to home, the redoubtable Margot Chapman Springer tells me that her school board has been bombarded by letters accusing her of teaching the joys of abortion and infanticide to her grade-nine girls. She was very uptight about it until it was noticed that not all of the letters were anonymous. Some bore names like O.D. Quaalude and H.I. Boghouse, which caused the Trustees to smell a rat, and the mystery was cleared up when it was discovered that all the envelopes were postmarked in Prince Albert.

I've always considered Zinger a relatively gentle soul, but Chappie insists that, if crossed, he's got a tough black streak in him. Don't we all? Chappie says he is, given the chance, "the sort of bastard who would light the string on a maiden's tampon." A loving reconciliation does not seem imminent.

Meanwhile, the political situation also seems to be disintegrating. Locally, rumour has it that Spence Tapsell is about to become a Dean. God forbid, but I fear the worst. His wife Muriel has been seen buying new hats, which is a very bad sign. Given a choice between Richard M. Nixon and Tapsell, I guess I'd choose Spence, but it would be a near thing. He remains the only man I know who can strut sitting down, and his politics seem to me a bit to the right of Genghis Khan.

On the broader scene, I continue to be appalled by the number of red-necks here who openly look forward to Quebec separating from Canada. Good riddance, many of them say. That talk scares the hell out of me. Little do they realize what agonies would be involved. The extreme Wasp "let-'em-split-quick" view seems to me just as loony and unrealistic as the view that René Lévesque is merely a harmless and lovable little gnome. Geez. Doesn't anybody around here READ anymore? The whole country is up for grabs, and most people want to treat it as a petty family squabble at a wienie roast.

At the moment, the French-Canadians appear self-absorbed and virtually self-sufficient. What we Anglos secretly fear and envy – note that a Uke like me is considered by a *Canadien* to be an "Anglo" – is French Canada's confident sense of identity. If they know nothing else, at least they know they're not Yankees. They damned well know who they are, which is more than you can say for most Canadians. But their sense of identity may be, as McLuhan suggests, increasingly narrow and tribal. Dangerous stuff, tribalism. If you've ever read Andrew Malcolm's *The Tyranny of the Group*, you'll remember his warning that "the tribe can be as oppressive a master as the machine."

Out here in the west, few people seem to know what, if anything, to make of Joe Clark. Trudeau's comeback, since the Quebec election, has been remarkable. Joe appears fumbling and uncertain. Jokes about Joe abound. He's an Albertan, a strange and Yankee-oriented breed by definition, but probably he fits less well in Alberta than anywhere else in Canada. Albertans like their politicians macho, as Christina McCall Newman said so well in a recent issue of *Saturday Night*. But macho is what Joe isn't.

Trouble with Joe, he was everyone's second choice for Tory leader, but almost no one's first choice. He won it because of what he was not. Not from Bay Street; not from Quebec; not a former Liberal; not an old man. When a party picks a leader for what he is not, it's in trouble. The Tories would have been better off to stick with Stanfield, or to go with Flora MacDonald – but unlike the British, we're still too immature for a female leader. My own choice, if I were giving advice to the Conservatives, would have been your Tiny Perfect One from Toronto, David Crombie. Not only is he a proven vote-getter in a city bigger than many provinces, but he is shrewd. He has charisma. He talks sense, and he talks tersely. Crombie impresses me as having very keen political instincts and an abundance of what can't be taught, savvy. Saw him again on TV the other night, and I'm not sure what it is that he's got, but he's got it. Moxie. He also has the best political campaign manager in Canada, Bill Marshall. Anyway, I hope the weakness of the federal Tories does not leave the field open to Trudeau by total default. When the Tories chose Joe Clark, they were looking desperately for a saviour, and they got a choirboy. Still, he could become prime minister. Ye gods.

What a preposterous country this is.

Regards,

Smig

From: Professor B.J. Gandy
Department of History
University of Saskatchewan

25 February 1977

My Dear McLaughlin,

Your letter of last December has been on my mind. It has left me aghast. I recall that you actually asked me what it meant to be a "conservative," what the term "Tory" means to me. I'm delighted to tell you, but somewhat taken aback that you should find it necessary to ask. The times are out of joint. I feel as though I were sitting down to a steak dinner at a cattle-breeders' convention and asked to give a talk on the meaning of vegetarianism. But such is the gap in the centre, the hiatus in the middle of the modern world. Everyone knows, or pretends to know, everything – except the basics. The contemporary world is not strong on basics. Which is why mental illness and idiocy abound. But that is another story.

The reason most people fail to comprehend true conservatism, McLaughlin, is that they fail to perceive the real nature of liberalism. Paradoxical? Well, our contemporary western world is so overwhelmingly liberal that trying to explain the concept of liberalism to a student is like trying to explain the concept of water to a fish. A fish doesn't know what water is, yet he knows nothing else. To some extent we are all finned and gilled.

You may find this insulting, dear boy, but let me push you back to basics. When we make our assumptions concerning the nature of man in society and politics, our choices are limited. Essentially there are only three paradigms, or patterns of thought. You need only three words as your touchstones:

– Individual
– Class
– Community

If you can see society as an aggregation of individuals, and men as discrete individual units, each clamouring to assert his fundamental "rights," including the right to compete with and trample his fellows, you are a liberal. Liberals exalt individualism.

If you view society as a materialist battleground of economic classes, and men primarily as members of classes engaged in a sordid struggle over property, you are an economic determinist, a Marxist.

But if you perceive society as an organism, as a living, growing thing in which the whole is greater than the mere sum of the parts, and see men not as isolated individuals or contending classes but as components of the social organism, having their worth and dignity in relation to the abiding human community, then you are a conservative, a Tory. A Tory asserts the persistence and primacy of community.

It is as simple as that. And yet, not so simple.

My distinguished colleague, the fine Tory historian W.L. Morton, has frequently observed that the Devil was the first Whig, and the ultimate Whig is the computer. Few people seem to appreciate the full sense of that pregnant statement. Allow me to interpolate.

In this excessively scientific age, with the blessings of science increasingly counterbalanced by the hideous and impersonal blights of technology, we live under a tyranny of "the facts." Every damned fool who scrapes through university courses learns some pseudo-science, some empiricism, and thinks he is educated if he has memorized some raw data, grubby facts, such as the date of the War of 1812. Empty, meaningless twaddle. Facts? Bullroar. It is fashionable to say that "the facts speak for themselves." But they do not. The facts are mute, dumb; they take on meaning and significance only in relation to human judgement, human values.

Fact: one fifth of Canadians live in poverty. That is statistically demonstrable. The question is, if I may put it so plainly, so what? What significance, what value shall we ascribe to this datum? We must decide. And we must decide not upon the basis of statistics but of morality. Is the extent of poverty inevitable or remediable? Desirable or deplorable? Damn it, is it good or bad?

Decisions on such matters cannot be made by science, by rude quantitative measurement, but only by qualitative value judgements. Values; there's the ticket. In my view, if a thing can be quantified, it is most probably not of fundamental importance. Who would try to measure Justice or Beauty? A work of art is not to be measured; would we apply a slide-rule to the Sistine Chapel? Ultimately it is the imaginative vision which sustains us, the glimpse of something higher, better.

And your liberal, McLaughlin, "the liberal enemy" seldom raises his eyes from his pathetic facts to seek the good. The more fool he. Fact-grubbers and "social scientists" bore me to distraction. They piddle about with their computers and their tiresome questionnaires for a "data base," but back away from value judgements like orthodox Jews from a ham, like canaries from a cat, babbling about "value-free science" and refusing to face the real questions concerning right or wrong, good or bad. Philistines.

Therefore, your silly liberal asks only the crude questions: "Is it efficient? Is it new? Will it work?" Despicable. "If it feels good, do it," is their only rule. "If it will work, let's make it, and never mind the social consequences," said innumerable committees of liberal politicians and scientists, blithely inventing such bountiful boons to mankind as the atomic bomb, strip mining, the national debt, and frozen plastic pizza.

Where did our modern world go wrong, McLaughlin? I'll tell you where. It went wrong in forgetting authority, the wisdom of experience, and tradition. The eternal verities, dear boy. Liberals, obsessed with empiricism, experiment, novelty, and "reason," believed they could dare anything. No holds barred. The emphasis on reason led to an insistence on total "freedom," unlimited liberty for every individual. And liberty became licence. I would contend that the only completely free man in the twentieth century was Adolph Hitler. What a sweet little rose he was. But he was "free," don't you see? He was free of all social restraint, custom, common sense or even conscience. Thus did the beguiling blossom of total individual liberty become the skunk-cabbage of evil.

No, McLaughlin, it won't do at all. Much of the world, much of human nature is, if unrestrained by tradition and authority, simply bad. But authority has everywhere been eroded in our limply permissive and libertarian society. Where, I ask you, is there to be found any respect for the lessons of experience? Where will we discover a vestige of authority? We live in a world in which children have no respect for parents, nor students for teachers. Union leaders have no authority over wildcat strikers, courts no authority over criminals, priests still less over parishioners. Even governments and the law itself are regarded as bad jokes to be flouted. The true conservative looks at all of this with dismay and loathing.

But as I recall you asked me what a Tory believes, and I have been expostulating upon what a Tory does *not* believe. Forgive me. I fear it is my habit, bred of long years of filling out the fifty-minute lecture period, to back into my subject gingerly rather than to dash into it headlong. Let me slice through to the heart of the matter.

—While naive liberals and socialists are Utopian, regarding human nature optimistically and man as "perfectible," your Tory believes that man is a fallen creature, possessed of a black streak a yard wide, and requiring the restraint of authority to keep him from slaughtering his fellows and debasing himself.

— Your blatherskite liberal rushes to embrace every change, every novelty, as "progress," but the Tory considers progress a nonsensical illusion. More bullroar.

— We Tories decry excessive individualism, insisting instead on the primacy of the social organism, the community. Society is perceived by the Tory to be made up of varying and unequal components, and the community should be organized hierarchically on the basis of recognized natural differences.

— Authority should be respected; scrutinized and limited, but respected. Law, order, stability and the historical wisdom of experience should temper the inclination toward experiment or rapid change.

Change should be accepted, but gradually and after due consideration.

— Cooperation between men and groups seems to us preferable to naked competition stained red of tooth and claw. Trust and mutual respect are required as the basis for cooperation, and if that trust is violated the conservative will invoke some traditional standards of conduct, some higher values and appreciation of "the good," those values being derived from the eternal founts of religion, custom, or morality.

— Moral relativism and the worship of gimmicks and techniques (such as bilingualism) are to be shunned as dread Whig diseases, just as Richard Nixon would be scorned by a true conservative as a base liberal thug.

— Unwritten codes of manners, morals and decency are probably more important than formal law. Good manners and gentility do more to ameliorate the human condition than politicians or public policies.

— No one should have unlimited "rights" to exploit his fellows or abuse the community. Although the rights and liberties of individuals are to be cherished, the genuine conservative will not hesitate to assert what George Grant has called "the right of the community to restrain freedom in the name of the common good."

— Although inequality is inevitable, privilege carries with it heavy social responsibility, and "noblesse oblige" is to be taken seriously by those fortunate enough to enjoy wealth or status.

And so, McLaughlin, we boil it down to the belief of conservatives in community, tradition, authority, cooperation, responsibility, manners, morality and the higher values over mere pragmatism. It is this Tory streak, of course, which primarily distinguishes Canadians from Americans, who are almost all liberals. Did you know that the two most accomplished scalliwag Tories of the nineteenth century, Disraeli and John A. Macdonald, corresponded on these matters and agreed entirely? Remember always that we poor humans are fallible, dear boy; we are highly risible and not perfectible.

But I see it is almost tea-time, and my musings and scoldings already have covered several pages. There are times, my dear McLaughlin, when political ideology seems to me less important than tea and good biscuits at four o'clock, and the agreeable certainty that once each week it will be Saturday afternoon.

Yours most sincerely,

B.J. Gandy

P.S., and just one further nudge at our topic.

Those of us who reject Utopian liberal idiocies should recall what my late friend Leonard Beaton argued in opposition to an ugly commercial scheme for urban redevelopment. His words might be the catechism of the true Tory. Beaton said, "In order to protect the community and prevent vulgarity, civilized people must impose their values on the merely rich." I like that. I like that immoderately. Civilization is a delicate and wondrous flower to be nurtured and protected against the barbarian hordes.

B.J.G.

To: Francis Z. Springer
Prince Albert, Sask.

1 March 1977

Dear Zinger,

I'm still hanging on tenter-hooks concerning my Innis manuscript and hoping against hope that within the near future I may yet have a book in print and a shot at tenure. Meanwhile, I pray for better medical news from Regina and I straggle along. Have caught up on my essay-marking as well as my lecture preparation. I'm spending most evenings writing and editing material for the textbook anthology with Cutty Cuttshaw. We hope to get rich. The midnight oil is aflame again.

When next we meet, I want to discuss with you a most unlikely series of letters I've received from old Gandy. Gradually I'm coming around to the realization that I may not be a liberal. The whole purpose of universities, I suppose, is to persuade people to re-examine their own assumptions and (just possibly) to change their minds. Few people ever do. Now that I may have to change my own mind, at the age of thirty-nine, I find it a most agonizing process. Having thought my way out of the individualist Chicago liberal ideology, I may have lost my intellectual rudder and come adrift, which is a helluva state for a professor.

At the moment I'm even prepared to believe that you possess an ostrich. If I can believe that, I can believe anything. How did you get out of jail? What does Mackenzie eat? What do you feed him?

Here I am trying to achieve tenure, to edit a textbook and to grapple with the assumptions of social science if not the eternal verities, and what really absorbs my mind is, what do you feed an ostrich? Does he eat jelly beans? Cashews? Tennis shoes? Won tons? Chicken fried rice??

Put me out of my misery with basic ornithological data, and send me the latest word on the penal system.

J.T.

From: Francis Z. Springer
Prince Albert, Sask.

5 Mar., '77

J.T.,

What does Mackenzie eat? Funny you should ask that. Apart from an old chesterfield, most of the stuffing of which he recently ate, I've had great difficulty in finding a suitable diet for him. When I take him out for a stroll on his leash, he evinces a certain fondness for hats. Loves to eat hats, a handy talent for some people after losing election bets, but decidedly inconvenient around the neighbourhood. Many's the hat he has beaked off the heads of unsuspecting local citizens, some of whom become quite huffy and shrill about it. Tends to shake them up a fair bit when an ostrich advances on them from behind and scoffs their chapeaux. There can't really be much nutritional value in hats, can there? I think he's part goat. Whatever.

Anyway, my attempts to get Mackenzie to eat birdseed or hamburger proved unavailing. He'd eat a certain amount of bridge mix or old poker chips, but not consistently. Probably his gastronomic peculiarities had something to do with the fact that he up and died last week.

It was just after the Winter Carnival, which you may remember we hold here every February on the river. It's what Stiffy calls the Winter Olympics for the Morally Handicapped. I wanted to enter Mackenzie in some of the races, but you'd be surprised how few events they have in Prince Albert for ostriches, drop-kicking of police sergeants excluded. They have snowball throws, ice-sculpture, ski-jumping, snow-shoe racing, speed-skating, muff-diving, and for local politicians the Men's Invitational Longjohn Open-flap Trap-door Numb-bumb Downhill Sledding-Without-Sled Event, as well as the Marian Engel Memorial Polar Bear Wrestling Climactic Contest. But nothing, absolutely nothing for ostriches. Bloody discriminatory.

Your average whooping crane can always count on a big government subsidy, but for ostriches, zilch.

Although they tried to bar Mackenzie from competition on the grounds that he was not a citizen or a landed immigrant, I hitched him up to a toboggan and ran him in the dog sled races. He showed a lot of early foot, particularly with the dogs snapping behind him. Carnivorous teeth, I find, are a considerable incentive to hustle one's tail. We easily outran all of the huskies and not a few of the snow-mobiles. I made a fair bundle on side bets, enough to tide me over some recent financial tribulations. By the way, Mackenzie's former owner once told me that my big bird has a distant relative named Ollie residing in the Toronto zoo. You should get Martin O'Malley of the *Star* (one of the good guys) to tell Larry the River to enter this relative in the trots at Woodbine. We'd clean up.

When the strain of racing and his somewhat eccentric diet proved too much (or too little) for Mackenzie, he up and died. Fell stone dead, he did, right after the Carnival, just when I was collecting several wagers and speculating that if I could teach him to skate he'd be a sensation with the Toronto Maple Leafs. He had a dynamite backhand.

Anyway, when Mackenzie went to his reward I was surprised how much I missed him, so I had him mounted and stuffed by a local taxidermist who does good work. Mac now is a very satisfactory coat rack. Inquiries as to whether I could have a similar procedure carried out on my mother-in-law proved fruitless, at least partly on the specious grounds that she is not yet deceased – contrary to all sound principles of natural justice. Guess she wouldn't make much of a coat rack anyway.

But poor Mackenzie is gone. Therefore, I am now casting about for another household pet. Any ideas?

Although they're rather hard to come by in the west, I thought a camel might be nice. Wouldn't be too much trouble; if they can go so long without drinking, camels might be less inclined to piss on the floor. Alternatively, a giraffe might suit, and be good company. Perhaps a small, female apartment-sized giraffe. I'm told that they have no vocal chords, a condition which appeals to me more than somewhat. Amazing how difficult it is to find non-garrulous female companionship here in P.A.

Yours zoo-ophiliacally,

Zinger

P.S.

On the other thing, about Gandy and so on: keep working, and persist in thinking like an economist if you must, but remember that if we were all rational economic-man calculating machines, there would be no good journalists, professors or artists. Individualism? Liberalism? Shitteree. Most people have never heard of these nutty categories. And recall, when we were undergraduates, Ken Buckley telling us to read Karl Polanyi's *The Great Transformation*, which demonstrates how market individualism breaks down the social fabric, how "market destroys community." As a zealous little student, you never could cope with that concept, could you?

If you were a rational individualist (or an island, Mr. Donne) you wouldn't be a romantic about universities; you wouldn't keep trying to protect what Abe Rotstein called "The Precarious Homestead." And we would not be in correspondence. To write letters is an attempt to transcend individual isolation, to reach out in the hope that we are not alone. A forlorn and misguided hope, I grant you. The trick is to hope sceptically and not naively. But if any of us really understood what we were doing to ourselves or to each other, we might turn up our toes like Mackenzie and get stuffed. Whatever.

I must get back to work and bang out another deathless editorial on freight rates or Barney will have my head. I'm off, like a bride's knickers.

Z.

From: Wilfred B. Twillington
Chiliast University Press

6 March 1977

Dear Professor McLaughlin,

I am now in a position to afford you further information concerning your manuscript.

The readers' reports on your second draft, which Mr. Williams and I have gone over very carefully, agree that several imperfections remain which must be attended to. Both readers agreed that your new additional chapter is not without interest. It contributes much toward our better understanding of the relationships between the work of Innis and of McLuhan.

It may, however, contribute too much. It may overshadow or overbalance the previous analysis of the relationships between the thought of Innis and of Veblen.

I will attach to this letter copies of the readers' assessments for your consideration. The upshot, I'm sure you will agree, is that the manuscript in its present form is unbalanced and too long. I'd be glad to discuss with you, at your early convenience, how this work might now be cut and trimmed into a more suitable length.

Yours sincerely,

Wilfred B. Twillington
Editor

To: Wilfred B. Twillington
Chiliast University Press

8 March 1977

Twilly,

You're having me on, aren't you, Wilfred old boy? You're pulling my leg and funnin' the old professor. I can take a joke, but this is ridiculous. Why do you want to kid me like this, Twilly? Why shit the troops? For a moment there I almost took you seriously as saying, "cut it down." You don't really mean that.

Well, I've read your note a second time – and a twelfth – with the realization slowly dawning on me that Groucho Marx you ain't. You're serious, aren't you, Twilly? You mean it.

Too long? Cutting and trimming? By God, lettuce head, you are the sonofabitch that ruined my entire Christmas holidays by telling me to expand it, to lengthen the book. And lengthen it I did, at no end of cost to my body and soul. You lop-eared lame-brained flabby-assed cretin, if you think for one moment I'd reduce that manuscript by one word, that I'd debase myself on the sacerdotal rug of your editorial office, you can blow it out your rear orifice. You will suffer the agonies of frying in hell with gelded polar bears shitting hot coals on your empty head before I will reduce my book by a single immortal syllable, before I will alter so much as a perfectly placed and exquisite comma.

Look, chowder-brain, you just ring up the typesetter and get this book into print pronto before I come over there and wire your genitals to the fire alarm and incinerate your putrid piles of ridiculous readers' reports. It's apparent that these incompetent assholes come out of the woodwork every two months to justify their assessors' fees by spouting off about things they don't understand, in entirely contradictory ways. This sort of asininity can't be taken seriously. I can't permit my life's blood and creative juices to be dribbled away into such idiotic puddles of unknowing.

Twilly, it's a book. Don't you see? It's a good book. It's a second draft that was done just as you and your cohort of anonymous addle-pated pusillanimous pundits said it should be done and re-done. What more do you want from me? What can I do now? I entreat you in all kindness, put me out of my misery; what further blood do you want to squeeze out of this stone?

Despairingly,

J.T. McLaughlin

To: Professor Jake Smigarowsky
Department of Political Science
University of Sask.

9 March 1977

Dear Smig,

I explained the situation to you as best I could on the phone the other night. I'm devastated. I don't know what to do or where to turn. Sometimes I really don't believe that all this is happening to me. For the past twenty-four hours I've been snarling at the kids; the dog cringes at my approach, and Patricia is convinced that I'm a failure and a donkey, unpublished and unpublishable. Trish hopes and assumes that anything I write will appear on page one of the *New York Times*, but when – after weeks of late night seclusion with a scotch bottle in my cellar study – I receive lurid and insulting rejection slips, my long-suffering wife begins to doubt that I am a genius. This sort of thing tends to erode the very fibre of domestic confidence and respect. I sense that Patricia may begin to question whether I can do it. Me, too.

What do I do now, Smig? What do I do??

Abjectly,

J.T.

P.S.

I'm in a position where I must consider everything and try anything. For some reason, Gandy has favoured me recently with his unlikely and upsetting opinions. Let's give it a shot: go down the hall, I beg you, explain the situation to Gandy, and see whether that wily old rogue can come up with any suggestions. Go, Smig; move. Au secours!

J.T.

From: B.J. Gandy
Department of History
University of Saskatchewan

12 March 1977

My Dear McLaughlin,

I do not recall that you have yet responded to my extended statement of the principles of conservatism. It will be a source of satisfaction for me to learn your reaction to my views on these issues and perceptions. I hope I made my opinions sufficiently clear. These are, it goes without saying, matters of consequence. In the intellectual community, we must be full and frank in the exchange of our conclusions lest ill-considered doctrines of a shallow and historically unsound nature capture the field by default.

You should, I believe, take a few weeks off to re-read Barrington Moore, (eschewing Macaulay and his ilk), as well as some Plato, Esmé Wingfield-Stratford, and Burke, in order to regain a balanced intellectual perspective on these troubled times. There are days, I confess, when I doubt that many people adequately appreciate the perilous state in which contemporary society finds itself. What a shame. Just a bit of judicious refreshment from the well-springs of history and the reflections of the great authors would do wonders to revive the modern spirit and re-kindle the dying flame of civilization. Keeping one's balance is all so simple, actually, if people would only pause to reflect on what the best of the western tradition has to teach us.

What I started to say was that, of our friend Smigarowsky, I have a high opinion. Good lad. Impatient, and given to over-simplification of issues, but his instincts are sound. Worries me a little, though, on occasion. Smigarowsky came panting into my office only yesterday with some risible tale concerning you and an editor chap. I'm not at all certain that he imparted the story to me clearly, but I think I caught his drift. You, I take it, submitted a manuscript. Readers' comments urged elaboration. You lengthened it and added a chapter. A good thing, too, I'm sure. But now, after lengthening, the present suggestion is that you reduce and shorten once again.

All of this seems to me no problem. I once had a colleague who went through a similar thrash. Lovely fellow in the Department of Classics, if I recall. Think his name was Conacher. Had much the same sort of problem. What I told him is what I propose to tell you. If the first draft was judged too brief, and if with the addition of a further chapter the result is now judged too long, you merely recognize the fallibility and inconstancy of human adjudication and resubmit the original version. This probably will not be noticed as being the original. Bash it in again as it was at first. Such gentle deception will enable you to buy time to consider, at your leisure, possible refinements. Meanwhile, a copy of the extra chapter should be submitted, as is, to at least one learned journal so that this additional work may appear in print as a separate article. Chances are, however, that the readers and editors are as exasperated by the prolonged procedures as you are, and may indeed accept the manuscript in its original form.

Try it. What can you lose? Meanwhile, I look forward to receiving your considered views on the assumptions underlying contemporary liberal economics, and to discovering whether the concept of community has impinged upon your consciousness as a result of my expostulations. These are matters, McLaughlin, which will repay attention and reflection. You seem to me, if I may say so, rather shaky on certain of these fundamentals, and I would be happy to learn that you are turning your mind to significant questions even if presently you are too enmeshed in the coils of ego and status to be capable of pursuing your education. You would be surprised, I think, what people are capable of learning after the age of thirty, or even sixty, if only by trial and error. Mostly error.

Yours most sincerely,

B.J. Gandy

To: Professor B.J. Gandy
Department of History
University of Saskatchewan

20 March 1977

Dear Professor Gandy,

I am exceedingly grateful to you for your letter of last week. Your suggestions, so simple and wry, are sufficiently wild that they just might work, or at least buy me a little time. I am going ahead with the re-submission of the manuscript in its pristine original form. My fingers are crossed, and I will let you know the results. I have also mailed a copy of the apparently superfluous chapter to the editor of *Canadian Economic History*. Lord knows I'm willing to try anything.

Please give my best regards to Smig when you see him. It was very kind of him to bring my desperate plight to your attention. His intercession and your thoughtful advice may yet save my bacon.

I hope you will pardon me if I do not comment at length on your most welcome letters and your remarkable statement concerning the nature of Toryism. At the moment I am too frenetically preoccupied with questions of publication and tenure to turn my mind to basic principles. Before we philosophize, we must first survive. But I do look forward to discussing these questions with you in the near future. In July, unless I fetch up unemployed, I expect to be in Saskatoon for a few days visiting Smig, and it would be a great pleasure to sit down with you for a serious discussion.

Meanwhile, please accept my repeated and warmest thanks for your help.

Yours sincerely,

J.T. McLaughlin

P.S.

Still, I remain puzzled by one thing. If Tories have such a coherent set of beliefs, and place such high value on the concept of "community," why has the Conservative Party remained out of office in Ottawa during most of this century, and why has the Conservative Party remained so weak in Quebec? I'd have thought that the Tory emphasis on tradition and community would appeal to Quebec most especially.

Can it be that principles and ideas are simply unimportant or irrelevant in Canadian politics?

J.T.M.

To: Francis Z. Springer
Prince Albert, Sask.

2 April 1977

Dear Zinger,

You would not believe the hassle I've had over my Innis manuscript. The Press seems to be staffed by nincompoops devoted only to keeping their jobs by dreaming up make-work projects for long-suffering scholars, and the more bizarre the projects, the better.

First the book was too short, then (months later) it was too long. Now, on the improbable advice of Gandy, I have re-submitted the manuscript in its original form, as it was way back in October, and am presently gnawing my fingernails as I anticipate their next verdict. If they catch me out in this deception they may toss out the whole project, and then where would I be? Up the flipping creek without tenure or a paddle, that's where. I'm sweating blood and shitting fudgesicles.

Paradoxically there has been a glimmer of good news from the editor of *Canadian Economic History*. He phoned me today "to express real interest" in publishing a chunk that I removed from the book during the last round, and I gather this piece just might appear in that blessed journal sometime before I reach the age of retirement. His phone call cheered me up a bit, even though nothing is yet definite.

However, the news from Regina is much less cheery. Dad is no better, in fact rather worse, and apparently popping pills like a rock musician. Poor old bugger; he's having it rough. I talked long distance to his physician the other night. The sawbones said that Dad was bearing up tolerably well, and that I should not visit Regina until later in the spring, after exams, on the theory that my sudden arrival might persuade Dad that he's worse than he really is. Take it easy, said the doc. Everybody keeps telling me to take it easy, but I'm wound up as tight as a four dollar watch. I'd like nothing better than to fly out and spend an inebriated weekend of disputation and dissipation with you, but exams are almost upon me. Marking is much the worst part of teaching.

Maybe I'll see you in July. Meanwhile, send me some good news of the true and the beautiful or supportive words from the gospel according to St. Dief.

Regards and stuff,

J.T.

From: Francis Z. Springer
Prince Albert, Sask.

8 Apr., '77

J.T.,

Good news? From here? Not bloody likely. Barney is yapping at me incessantly to dummy up editorials on how we love the French and want Quebec to stay in; Chappie has garnisheed my wages for non-support; I am suffering from an onslaught of bill collectors; the province is seized by drought; even the rigid Mackenzie seems to be sulking and moulting under the coats and hats, which seems un-grateful after all I did for him. And ominous symptoms of semi-acute alcoholism seem to be emanating from my ravaged liver. I think I liked it better being in jail. (They gave me a suspended sentence and six months' probation.)

The only good news is about Stiffy, who seems to be having a glorious time in the hospital. He says it's swell. Last week he came down with some mysterious stomach complaint, enough to get him off work and into the serenity of a hospital bed, but not enough to daunt his high spirits. I'd like to know what kind of pills he's on; his eyes gleam wickedly. Apparently some of the younger nurses took a great shine to him, as a lot of well-intentioned local folks do when they get a chance to be patronizing and condescending to Indians, and when some bath attendant or bed-pan toter spread the word that the evil little fellow was equipped with the biggest schlong north of Moose Jaw, he became an instant sensation and the institutional pet.

A bevy of girls seem to be in constant attendance at his bedside day and night. I don't know when he gets any sleep. They couldn't care less about his belly ache (they vie with one another to sneak him extra victuals, candy, and flasks of vodka), but they sure care a lot about his remarkable tent-pole. Rows of nurses are often lined up all the way down the corridor to view it. The tittering is something wondrous to behold. Admittedly Stiffy has a notable horn, but I do think the girls get a bit carried away. After midnight I'm told there are veritable traffic jams, and his room is like a sultan's harem.

Stiffy is the centre of such lavish and adulatory female attention that he swears he never wants to leave the hospital, and it's almost impossible to fight your way through the rapturous crowds of quiff to visit him. When I walked in the other day there was one nurse with her head under his covers, three others waiting to settle a bet concerning his manly dimensions with a yardstick, and another score of giggling quail in white lurking about in hopes that he would autograph their panties. I've never seen so much moist lingerie flaunted since a rain storm blew the roof off the burlesque house.

"Stiffy," I said, "your mythical proportions have now reached mythical proportions." "Yup," he said, "it's fatiguing, but it is rewarding. With a little luck and some benzedrine, and if the doctors continue to be perplexed about my gut, I may be able to stand at stud in this hospital for another month. You meet a better class of people here than you do back at the newspaper. I'm seldom lonely." "But Stiffy, you may wear yourself out and have a serious physical collapse." "Nice of you to be concerned, Francis," (he calls me Francis just to irritate me), "but where better to have a physical collapse than in a hospital? And in what more noble cause? Besides, I see myself as a goodwill ambassador from my people, doing my own poor bit to improve racial relations and reduce tensions among these paleface ladies who have hitherto been deprived of a proper understanding of native ways. You've heard of Sitting Bull? I hope to go down in history as Tumescent Bull, a potent symbol of upward mobility to my tribe." "How?" "Don't 'how' me, you envious honky bigot." "No, I mean how do you intend to keep it up? At this rate you may soon be squeezed dry. You may become known as Little Flaccid Horn, and never rise again." "Leave me to worry about that, Francis, and just you bring me some ginseng root and a bucket of oysters tomorrow, O.K.?"

"I thought you told me the food here was excellent," I rejoined, trying to steer the conversation in a more temperate direction. "What do you like best?" "Best? That's a tough question, Keemosabe. I think best I like the blondes in the black garter-belts, although there is much to be said for a large brunette in a red garter-belt who comes in just after midnight. Redheads I prefer *au naturelle*, as M. Lévesque might put it. Now leave me. I must tend to my flock. Visitors tend to cramp my style and inhibit the little darlings."

It was clear to me that my old buddy was beyond redemption, and equally clear to me that he was not going to offer to share his heady new-found largess. As I slouched out I was accosted by a whopping great giantess of ill-favoured visage and stern demeanour. This, I gathered, was the Head Nurse, a formidable old party who takes a dim view of Stiffy and his disruption of her staff. "You a friend of that dirty little Injun?" she demanded. I admitted it. "Well you tell him that if he doesn't leave my girls alone I will personally perform a permanently debilitating operation on him with a rusty scalpel, without anesthetic. You take my meaning? He will be singing to the Great Manitou as a boy soprano. You tell him that."

Now I, of course, pride myself on being a consummate diplomat, so I attempted to smooth her feathers by complimenting her on the excellence of her staff and reminding her that poor Stiffy is a sick man. I also inquired about his diagnosis, and what treatment the doctors had prescribed. "Well," she admitted, "there does seem to be some kind of stomach problem, but the doctors aren't sure what. I believe we will have to take particular care of his diet. Meanwhile, just to be prudent, I've given orders that he be given frequent enemas and fed only rectally." "Rectally?" I exclaimed. "Surely you can't mean that!" "Oh but I do, I do indeed. And it seems to be working, too. Why, this morning his arse fairly snapped at the toast."

You can see that Stiffy has had a lot of excitement recently. I'll try to find some oysters for him tomorrow, and keep you posted on his progress. I can foresee a bit of a dust-up between himself and the Head Nurse. This may be the greatest local skirmish since the Battle of Batoche in '85. I hope he doesn't get himself hanged.

Never underestimate the aroused Redskin.

Zinger

P.S.

Isn't it ironic? They hanged Riel, but they invite Lévesque to Federal-Provincial conferences.

Thus does the world wag.

Z.

From: Professor B.J. Gandy
Department of History
University of Sask.

9 April 1977

My Dear McLaughlin,

I must say that I find your questions refreshing, but your ignorance astounding. It's a good thing you know some economics, for it is clear that you are as innocent as a new-born kitten on the subject of history. Why have Tory principles appealed so little to the Canadian electorate in this century, and why still less to voters in Quebec? Not an entirely simple question, but one which I can handle with dispatch.

A phenomenon I regret most particularly, McLaughlin, is how few members of the Conservative Party have been proper Tories. Part of your answer may indeed lie there, but that is another story.

To all intents and purposes, the Quebec wing of the party was destroyed after the death of Sir John A. One factor which hastened its demise was precisely its emphasis on the concept of community. The party clung to the correct principle, but applied it wrongly. Too simplistically. From the passing of Macdonald in '91 to Mr. Diefenbaker's strident insistence on "One Canada," Conservatives invariably have stressed the unity of the society and the primacy of the organic community. Inconveniently, this assertion has rendered them blind to the possibility – the reality – that the Canadian community is not one, but two. While the Liberals since Laurier have acknowledged the duality of the nation and attempted to work out a sense of partnership with French Canada, the Conservatives evidently have preferred to pretend that only a single community exists. Bullroar. We are Canadians, and we are two.

The Conservatives' well-known tendency, in the face of Liberal cunning, to circle the wagons and shoot inward has resulted in the internecine slaughter of many national leaders, but no less important has been the fact that not one of the Tory leaders has been French

Canadian. Link this with the hanging of Riel, plus the enthusiasm for conscription in two world wars, and we have no difficulty seeing how the Conservative Party has managed to antagonize Quebec and to cripple itself. Thus the party in this century has contrived to march briskly into most federal elections with some seventy-five Quebec seats already lost. Cut off a finger and then wonder why your hand hurts, eh?

We need not belabour the obvious success of the Liberals in wooing Quebec and using that province as the pillar of power. What is less often remarked, I think, is how the Grits (and many scholars who should know better) have sold us a bill of goods about English-French differences making this a "precarious" nation, difficult to govern, and about to fly apart at any instant. Horsefeathers. These fatuous numbies have persuaded us that we should be cautious and timid, pushing ourselves to the point of national paranoia and seeing ourselves as "victims." Will we survive? Should we not quake and quiver over national unity? After all, our nationhood is "precarious." How I hate that word! Margaret Atwood observes, apropos our pervasive national masochism, that if *Moby Dick* had been written by a Canadian, the tale would be told not from the perspective of Captain Ahab, but of the whale. It's enough to make one cringe.

Holy harpoons, of course we have problems. But "precarious?" Surely this is a gross exaggeration, if not silly. Canada is one of the largest and richest nations of the world, lavishly endowed with resources, and enjoying one of the highest standards of living on the globe. We have never had a civil war. Apart from a pathetic handful of men with pitchforks in 1837, and a tiny band of gallant Métis with buffalo rifles in 1885, we have never seen anything approaching a revolution. Give or take a few mad Fenians, and a brief foray in 1812 by some half-hearted Yankees who couldn't cope with Laura Secord's cow, we have never been invaded. Our politics display a striking pattern of national liberal dominance, with benighted liberals prevailing most of the time in *both* our major parties, and the arrogant Grits straddling the extreme middle, out of office for only six of the forty-two years since 1935.

To any sane observer, McLaughlin, this evidence would suggest that Canada is one of the most secure and solid nations, one of the most maddeningly immovable states, probably one of the most glacially boring, docile, inert, and altogether catatonic societies ever known to man. Gibraltar should be so tottering. But, precarious? Tell *that* to the Italians, the Ethiopians, or the Israelis – but stand well back when you say it.

Certainly there is English-French tension in Canada, the quandary of Quebec, the spectre of distintegration which has haunted our national life. The situation is serious, I agree. But after decades of paralytic fear about "national unity," the penultimate disaster befell us with the election of an avowedly separatist government in Quebec.

And the result has been . . . what? The fearsome separatist fanatics seem to me like wet puppies. They shake all over us, but continue to wag their tails. They now propose "sovereignty – *with* association," an "independent" Quebec – *but* sharing with Canada a common market, a common currency, and probably common defence arrangements. In other words, separatism without separation. Let's be apart, but with the umbilical cord unsevered. Undoubtedly, there may yet be troublesome consequences, but a cynic might be pardoned if he found the situation a trifle incredible, just a touch risible. For here we find in the "sovereignty – *with* association" proposal a phenomenon not unlike a husband and wife, after a prolonged and acrimonious divorce, solemnly deciding to live together in the same house.

Harold Innis was right. The principal threat to our "precarious" national existence is that we may die laughing.

Let us hope, my dear McLaughlin, that whatever happens to our self-deluding and lunatic country, we will not lose sight of our principle of shared community and partnership, or our sense of humour.

With repeated best wishes for the success of your book, I remain,

Yours most sincerely,

B.J. Gandy

To: Francis Z. Springer,
Prince Albert, Sask.

11 April 1977

Dear Zinger,

About Stiffy. I'm more than somewhat perplexed by one aspect of your story. There's one thing I rather wonder about, just one thing I've got to ask you.

You know how most men, I guess about 99 per cent of men if they were honest, wonder somewhere deep down about their prowess, whether they are adequate where it counts, or adequate enough. How does it stack up relatively – you know. I mean, in all the dirty books I've read and in all the pornography I've looked at, the one thing that's never made clear or specific is, how big is Big?

Is it really true that Stiffy is so formidably endowed? Look, will you tell me, just how long IS it??

Just interested, you understand.

J.T.

From: Francis Z. Springer,
Prince Albert, Sask.

14 Apr., '77

J.T.,

Yeah, I understand. It is indeed a subject which almost all chaps find of some passing interest. And certainly Stiffy is remarkable.

What you want to know is, how big, right?

Well, if I were to be factual and scientific about it, if you were to press me for precise dimensions, I'd say it is about – well, you know, it's somewhere on the order of, or, more exactly, well, how shall I put it?

About this big.

Does that help?

Zinger

From: Doctor R. Woodley
Regina, Sask.

15 April 1977

**TELEGRAM**

PROFESSOR MCLAUGHLIN STOP COME TO REGINA AT ONCE
STOP I REGRET TO INFORM YOU THAT YOUR FATHER PASSED
AWAY SUDDENLY TONIGHT STOP I HAVE YOUR MOTHER
UNDER SEDATION PENDING YOUR ARRIVAL STOP

DR. R. WOODLEY

From: Professor Jake Smigarowsky
Department of Political Science
University of Saskatchewan

21 April 1977

Dear J.T.,

I was most extremely sorry that we had to meet in such strained and melancholy circumstances as your father's funeral. We scarcely had a chance to talk, bucko. Ruth joins me in extending our deepest sympathy. Your Dad was a fine man. We didn't agree on much, but he was always jaunty and straightforward. I respected him. He was always proud of you, and you have abundant reason to be proud of him. He had balls. Plus compassion. What more could be asked?

You may not know that I visited him in Regina and had a chat with him only two weeks before his passing. He told me that I was an ignorant ivory-tower Bohunk, and a "wrong-headed sillybugger altogether," but he gave Ruth a recipe for his Saskatoon-berry liqueur and me a pair of Canadian Legion cufflinks. I appreciated that. He talked enthusiastically about your children, his grandchildren, and how they saw through the difficulties and improbabilities of the generation gap. He connected directly with them and they with him, and he rejoiced in that unspoken communication. Generation gaps occur only in twos, not in threes. Every third generation understands the first. In the Hebraic faith, a friend tells me, if the first generation brings forth a Rabbi, the second generation will produce a shyster lawyer, the third a psychiatrist who understands everything. And the fourth generation is likely to include another Rabbi who forgives everything. We Ukrainians have a saying that fathers and sons invariably misunderstand each other because they are rivals. The measure of tension is often the measure of love.

I am sorry that you had to hurry back to Toronto to attend to exams. We'd have been glad to have you come up to Saskatoon with us for a few days. Today is one of those incredibly glowing, warm and fresh afternoons when all of the girls on the campus look as though they had bought new brassieres and just washed their hair. Gandy sat on the steps of the Arts Building, surrounded by laughing students, and even Tapsell bought a round at the Faculty Club while miscuing and sinking his own white ball at billiards. Crocuses are in bloom, and for a minute there when the breeze blew from the river I thought I saw W.O. Mitchell's wind.

You ought to come back later this summer for a real visit. We could drive by Timmie's house and remember old times. We could remember the wonder of the breasts that we first touched in the back seats of Chevrolets by the river. Memories might stir of mickeys of cheap rye under tables at dances, four-in-the-morning discussions of the eternal puzzlements, how to disguise pimples on the nose with Clearasil, whether draft beer was preferable to bottled at the Embassy Hotel, and whether George Britnell would ever get to Confederation in his historical lectures on Canadian politics. We could reflect on a lot of things, and almost feel young again.

Do come.

Ruth sends her love.

With sympathy,

Smig

To: Francis Z. Springer
Prince Albert, Sask.

22 April 1977

Dear Zinger,

Smig says he told you of my father's sudden death, but of course you could not leave Prince Albert for such a frivolous ceremony as a funeral. I hoped and expected to see you; I should have known better. I phoned you that Friday night, but there was no answer. Busy, busy, eh, Zinger? Certainly no time to come to Regina. Shit, man, I could have used some help. Don't know how I would have got through it all without good old Smig and Ruth. Even though I was in a daze most of the time, I was awfully grateful to have them there.

My mother, predictably, fell apart completely and blithered incoherently all weekend. I still feel rocked and stunned by it all. It takes a while for the numbness to wear off. What I'm going to do about Mom, I'm damned if I know. The prospect of her coming here to live with us sends shivers down my spine. She'd drive Patricia mad in no time.

From my present perspective, with piles of hundreds of exams staring me in the face, things look pretty bleak.

Anyway, thanks for nothing. In your next reincarnation maybe you'll be something more responsive and mobile, like a parking meter.

Up yours, sport.

J.T.

From: Francis Z. Springer
Prince Albert, Sask.

25 Apr., '77

J.T.,

My querulous friend, you got one thing straight, at least. Yes, you should have known better. Whatthehell.

I'll happily cross the street to see a friend. I will also, if pressed, cross two streets to see a friend in need, provided he's not too embarrassing and maudlin about it. But I will not, willingly, move a muscle or shift a buttock to attend a funeral. Any funeral. Don't much fancy them. They tend to depress me.

I am sorry that your Dad died. I'm sorry that you're sorry, as well you might be. The old boy did a lot for you, and was not an entirely contemptible old geezer. But personally I did not much get on with him, and it's my strong impression that you didn't either. Don't string me a line, J.T. If you had wanted, really wanted, to see him since Christmas, you would have hauled your filial ass to Regina before the praying and burying commenced, while he was still alive. You did not. Oh I know about the doctors saying not to be alarmed and not to alarm him, but you knew the score, and you'd have found some pretext to be on the scene if you'd wanted to and it had suited your convenience.

I know your response: pressure of work; manuscripts; tenure-schmenure. The bottom line is that you did not come west, all year, because you did not want to be bothered, and because you blithely assume that all right-thinking citizens should show up in Toronto. Which he did. Enough said.

If you can visit Prince Albert, I'll be glad to see you. In fact if you can visit Saskatchewan, I'll meet you halfway, like Saskatoon, but if you think I'm going to drive, walk or fly all the way to Regina for the sake of wringing a hanky with you and sniffing the lilies, you've got another think coming.

I can see it all now – you and the soulful Smig pulling long faces and wallowing in self-pity and pseudo-sorrow, the funereal organist pulling out all the stops while you indulge in a tearful singalong to the tune of "Nearer my God to Thee." What a mockery. Life is for the living, and funerals are for the living. The dead don't get much of a break. No, invite me to a barbecue, to a picnic, a political rally or to a booze-up, but don't invite me to a funeral. I'm not available.

And I don't like to be scolded.

Zing it.

Zinger

To: Francis Z. Springer
Prince Albert, Sask.

29 April 1977

Dear Zinger,

Maybe I had that coming, but I still think you are a clod not to have come to Regina that weekend. Being a "private" person is one thing, but being a hermit is another. I'm not certain what the centre of the universe is, but I'm pretty sure it is not Prince Albert. If you choose to sequester yourself in the boonies, in the back of beyond, that's your business, but it may not be surprising if your friends expect you to venture beyond your northern igloo once or twice each decade, at least, to observe the social amenities and common decencies. What have you got to lose? Are you afraid of the outside world? I wish you could see your way clear to bend just a little.

Why don't you consider moving to Toronto? The big town is where the action is. Chappie would take a different view of things in Toronto, I'll bet. With your experience, you could easily catch on here and get a job. You could live very comfortably. We could have long drinking sessions and visit back and forth and swap lies every week. Why not shake loose from Prince Albert and come to Toronto? Even Patricia, who thinks you are a bit of a strange nerd altogether, says she'd be happy to see you here. Toronto is where it's at.

And where I'm at, this week, is still struggling with late exam returns, trying to get back to editing the textbook with Cutty, and hoping against hope that I may be able to get away with my latest scam with the University Press concerning the book manuscript, which may make or break me. My fingernails are now gnawed down to the quick.

The quick and the dead. There's the essential contrast, right? My father is no longer among the quick, and I feel enormously depressed and guilty about it all. With you, F.Z., I won't pretend that Dad was in my thoughts all the time, or that I did all I could, or should. It's true Dad and I seldom saw eye to eye. Clearly we did not have frequent heart-to-hearts these past few years, or in fact since I went to graduate school. But I feel badly about it all.

I feel about him as I felt about an old elm tree in front of our house. The elm tree and I seldom had much conversation. Usually I scarcely noticed it; took it for granted. But when it got the blight and had to be cut down, I had an acute sensation of loss, a feeling that something was missing from the front of my life. I was a little less shaded, a little diminished, more naked. And full of regret. Elm trees and life now seem to me more insubstantial and more precious.

You are an ornery sonofabitch, Zinger, but may your beer never lack froth.

J.T.

From: Francis Z. Springer
Prince Albert, Sask.

5 May, '77

J.T.,

I'm genuinely sorry about your father's passing, but you do go on, don't you? Elm trees, yet. Ticking off attendance and calling the roll at funerals. I may throw up. You were no better a son than you ought to have been. You were more dutiful in your obeisances at the death than you were in the life, so don't try to con a con man. I've been there. It smarts, I grant you, but the situation is not unfamiliar.

My own father and I had some difficulties of communication and some brisk passages at arms. Stiffy (now safely out of hospital but still a little queasy of gut) tells me that his father threw him out when he evinced a desire to learn reading and writing at the white man's school. His papa was probably right, but television would have got to Stiffy in the end. We all do what we must, and ultimately it doesn't much matter. Whatthehell.

The sudden passing of my own Dad, some years ago, caused me a few twists and squirms, I admit. At one point I was so ridden by the guilts and the hoo-haws in the night that I consulted a spiritualist, a medium. Wonder of wonders, this old gypsy seer established contact with Pop in the great graduate school in the sky. "Are you O.K. there Dad?" I asked. "He says he's O.K." "I mean, ask him if he's happy, if he's all right or in pain." "He says he's just fine," the medium repeated. "*Dead*, of course, but otherwise just fine." "Ask him whether I can do anything for him, if he wants anything." "He says if you didn't do beans for him before he went six feet under, it's a little late to be solicitous. But he says that if you insist, you could give the medium $500 for inter-galactic postage, and maybe send up some corned beef and cabbage. With mustard. Creamed cabbage, and make sure the beef is lean." "That's my Dad, all right! Ask him whether he has regrets, or whether he misses anything he used to have here." "The spirit of your dear departed one says that he misses flowers, and tankards of ale, young girls skipping, and the song of meadowlarks on the prairie." "Meadowlarks? Tell him I thought he was tone deaf." "The departed says that he was never a big fan of Bach or Beethoven, but that all these incessant harps and choruses of angels are driving him bonkers." "Does he want to tell me anything most particularly? Does he have any advice for me? Mention to him that I'm at a loss as to what to do, what to believe." "He says you will persist in believing what you want to believe, and doing what you intended to do, but that you might consider letting more out from inside, giving more vent to your emotions, doing more hugging and smiling, and maybe giving your mother a rap in the chops for being such a surly bitch."

Of course there can be no doubt, J.T., that I had established a fortuitous contact with my old Dad in the Big Beyond, but in retrospect I'm not sure what good it did either one of us. Even the corned beef proved difficult to transmit, so I felt obliged to dispatch it myself more immediately in the here and now.

Another thing. Dad never did mention how much he enjoyed his funeral.

Look, there's not much we can do about this birth and death stuff except to enjoy the interval. Even that is not always easy. For my own part, I don't want to hear about your soul-searching over your Dad, who was an amiable old coot but a bigot and a fool – very much like you, in fact, much as you try to hide it. And if you want to hear from trouble, let me report that Chappie hung up in my ear when I phoned her the other night, that I'm broke, and that I got fired again this week. Turfed out on my ass, by God, with no mention of severance pay. I'm beginning to get the impression that this job may not be steady.

Barney, I may have mentioned, has been under pressure from Dowie, and bugging me to churn out more editorials about how we must overcome Quebec separatism and establish better relations between English and French Canada. I must have written six or eight breathless and bleeding-heart pieces on the subject recently, and had pretty much run dry when it suddenly occurred to me to make use of the innumerable volumes the paper receives for review, and to award book prizes for adroit translations of familiar sayings and slogans from the French. And vice versa. Might help to get the school kids involved and practising their language arts. So with Barney's consent I ran a big half-page announcement of the contest, stressing the importance of national unity and bilingualism, as well as prizes. Neat idea, everyone said.

At first the results, in terms of numbers of entries, were disappointing. Therefore, I ran the announcement again the following weekend and for good measure included an example of an artful translation. Maybe I should have checked it with Barney first. My example ran like this:

> Il y avait un plombier, François,
> Qui plombait sa femme dans le Bois.
> Dit-elle, "arretez!
> J'entends quelqu'un venait."
> Dit le plombier, en plombant, "C'est moi."

Now that, as you know, is a fine and authentic bit of the French oral tradition. It is in fact included in G. Legman's scholarly compilation, *The Limerick* (Bell Publishers, New York, 1969, second edition, p. 13). Stiffy liked it. I liked it. Many high school students of French wrote in to say they liked it. But then some thoughtless and excessively literate bastard translated it for Dowie. He didn't like it. Dowie doesn't know much, including French, what's funny, or his ass from his elbow. Still, if someone draws him a diagram, he can tell when he's been had. He bounced me out on my ear.

Unemployment is bloody inconvenient, particularly when you have debts to pay and Chappie to placate, but at least I can take solace in knowing that I did my earnest bit to assist the cause of national unity. I am, like Louis Riel, misunderstood and a martyr. Damned if I can see what harm there was in it. Here is Dowie, like most other newspaper publishers in the country, cheerfully printing advertisements for guns, cigarettes, snowmobiles, and intimate products coyly related to feminine hygiene – like "Pussy Pure" and "Twinkle Twat" – plus other blessings of modern civilization, and then, inexplicably, he takes violent exception to a harmless bit of folk verse. Bloody unjust. I was only being playful, like a breeze under a Scotsman's kilt, and didn't mean to get anything rampant, but here I am on the bread line again. It's all such shitteree.

I'm going out to get drank, and to hell with it.

Zinger


P.S.

I forgot that your French is about as good as Dowie's or Dief's, maze chair Canajjeeyans, so I will add the original:

> There was a young plumber of Leigh
> Who was plumbing a girl by the sea.
>   Said she, "Stop your plumbing,
>     I hear someone coming!"
> Said the plumber, still plumbing, "It's me."

Keep your plunger up.

Z.

To: Francis Z. Springer
Prince Albert, Sask.

11 May 1977

Dear Zinger,

I am genuinely sorry to hear that you got fired again. Things are tough all over, but you do persist in sticking your addled head smack into Dowie's noose. Probably it will all blow over, though.

By the way, I looked up the Legman collection of limericks, and I couldn't find any "reverse" ones in it. You know, the "backwards" kind that I mentioned to you way back last fall, with an example of a classic one by Thurber. If you're so flipping smart, write me one of those. But for kristsake keep it out of the newspaper.

While you have some leisure on your hands, this might be a good time to shape up and get some exercise. You'd feel much better for it. Probably you should cool it a bit on the booze, and cut back on cigarettes. If you could pull yourself together a bit, Chappie might find you more tolerable. And I wish you'd give some serious thought to leaving Prince Albert altogether and moving to Toronto. Come for a visit, at least. It would be nice to see you.

Cutty and I are getting on with our textbook anthology, but recently I've not heard a peep out of the Press about my Innis manuscript. Spin a few prayer wheels for me, O boney Buddha of the west.

Regards,

J.T.

From: Mother,
Regina, Sask.

14 May 1977

John dear,

I do wish you would come home to Regina for a few days to help me
sort out some of your father's affairs. Even the income tax form
confused me and I had to get help. Since Dad passed on I just can't
seem to cope. Everything seems so much more complicated and
costly than it used to be. I've hired a boy to come and cut the grass
every week, but now he tells me that we need a new lawn-mower.
How much do they cost? What kind should I buy? Dear me, I'm
sure I'll never understand about machinery. And I don't have any
pep or energy. Most days I just don't know what to do with myself.
There's absolutely nothing any good on the television anymore, is
there? And many of our old friends have died or moved away. Some
of the neighbours who still drop in are such *limited* people, aren't
they? Nothing to talk about. Why don't you send me a copy of that
book you were writing? You did promise. I'm sure I would find that
interesting. Anyway, do try to come out here for a few days very
soon. Or perhaps you would prefer me to come to Toronto for a few
weeks? I really don't have much to do here that's very pressing at the
moment. Except for the lawn-mower. And that awful Mr. Trudeau
keeps pushing all the prices of things up and making matters worse.
Things were much better when Mr. Diefenbaker was in office.

Love,

Mother

To: Mother,
Regina, Sask.

18 May 1977

Dear Mom,

For a number of reasons it's not entirely convenient to have you come here at the moment. It's an easy trip by plane, you know, and we do look forward to having you here for a good visit quite soon. But right this month wouldn't work out all that well.

However, I will definitely try to nip out to Regina for a few days, possibly in June. Certainly by July. If you send me any of Dad's accounts or financial statements, or even the income tax information, I'll be glad to sort it all out. The house is paid for, of course, and we went over the company's pension provisions when I was there in April. Clearly you have no financial worries. Buy any kind of lawnmower you like. Maybe electric.

But the important thing for you to do is keep active. Why not take up a nice hobby, or do some sort of community volunteer work? We've got to keep you stirred up and vital. Any time we've talked by phone recently you've sounded a bit draggy, or half asleep. Activity; that's the thing. And do not go on and on about how old you are or how boring everything is. You are not old. You are not even seventy, for Pete's sake. Why, just the other night on TV I saw a little old lady of eighty-four who was very spry, so spry that she played a tuba and tap danced at the same time, which tells you something about how to fight off the years, as well as something about the decline of western civilization.

Keep busy, and I'll see you as soon as I can.

Love,

J.T.

From: Mother,
Regina, Sask.

23 May 1977

John dear,

I'm sure I would not dream of visiting you in Toronto for even a few days if I'm not welcome. It just seemed to me Patricia might want some help with the housekeeping and the cooking since she isn't very good at it. But I'll make sure you get some good square meals and proper nourishment when you come to Regina which I trust will be very soon. I should point out that I certainly do keep busy, and have plenty to do without taking up a musical instrument, particularly the tuba. But I will never understand why you keep on making snide remarks about western civilization just because you've moved east for a few years. You were born out here, remember that, and westerners are every bit as civilized as easterners. Maybe more so, as I'm sure your father would have agreed. It won't be the same without Dad, of course, and he always did enjoy the drive, but if I come by plane perhaps I wouldn't be too much trouble if I came to Toronto next Christmas?

Love,

Mother

From: Francis Z. Springer
Prince Albert, Sask.

25 May, '77

J.T.,

You're a real fountain of advice and moral exhortation, aren't you? A jim-dandy little helpy-elf trying to uplift the underprivileged and the downtrodden. I find it nauseating. Another load of your unctuous advice I do not need. Zing it.

What is all this crap about smoking and drinking and exercise? I'll just bet, you hypocritical creep, that you had a cigarette burning and a scotch at your elbow while you wrote that fatuous letter, not true? But it would be grand if I practised abstinence, while you continue to suck it all up in a two-fisted professorial manner, tut-tutting at the lower orders. You're incredible.

Someone did ask me recently what I do for exercise, and I allowed that I wriggled my ears once a month in parlour games, mostly beer-parlour games, and have a very stiff action on my cigarette lighter. The fact is that I get rather less exercise this spring than I did last fall. Used to be that I walked, most every night, to the bar at the Marlborough, and back home. Lately I find that I still walk to the bar, but usually have to be carried home, a considerable conservation of energy but a decrease in exercise. I feel much the better for it, except in the mornings, which don't count. Who wants to live forever?

Particularly in Toronto. The idea of anyone living there voluntarily strikes terror to my heart. We've been all through this before. You say that there are beautiful tree-lined streets in Toronto, except for the areas devastated by pollution and Dutch elm disease; I say there are trees outside my door, endless acres of honest-to-God forest just north across the bridge, and a lovely river just outside my window. You say that you want Jossy and Rob to have the chance to be members of a "smart" riding club; I say that John can borrow a horse any time from a neighbour at the end of our street. You say that you want your kids to have all the cultural advantages of a major urban centre, and you like to go to the theatre; I say that your kids have all the cultural advantages of louder rock stations and more commercial TV from Buffalo, plus easier access to dope pushers in the school yards, as well as larger and more garish shopping plazas to hang around. To support these bizarre habits you have been slugging your guts out every night over a steaming typewriter in your basement while neither you nor Patricia has been inside of a theatre in months. We have nice basements in P.A. There are, of course, better restaurants in Toronto, but your rents and mortgages are so high that most people regard a trip to McDonald's as a big night out.

The bottom line is, though, that you as an "intellectual" think it is important to live in the big town where all the "smart" folks are, exchanging incestuous opinions within a two-mile radius as to what is "in" or "out" this week, opinions based on slavish agreement with three columnists, a TV "personality" and two precious magazine editors whose horizons range from Queen St. to Bloor. The truth is that Toronto is a tiny village of self-adulatory navel-gazing geeks who run in herds, speak in pseudo-hip clichés, and spend most of their time congratulating each other on being only six months (if not ten) behind the other phonies who set the fads and fee-ash-yons in London and New York. Do you honestly think that REAL people would live, willingly, in Toronto? The truth is that you can't understand anything, not anything, if you attempt to live there. Certainly nothing serious. Honest-to-God people have problems and perceptions, shifts of mood and sentiment, but in Toronto all you have is petty gusts of bad taste pushed by CBC producers, gossip columnists, temporary paper millionaires and other imbeciles, marginally and tentatively associated with any one of the three sexes, prancing on platform shoes across a desert of boutiques and asphalt. A freak show. Coney Island without the beach. Yech. Little theatres producing "reality" in old factories; new factories producing non-reality theatrically; theatrical people producing candy-floss imitations of reality, with a little violence in the streets and subways for the savour. Whatever.

My share, you can have, and welcome.

Here's a better idea. Instead of me moving to Toronto, why don't you give up your pathetic quest for tenure and move to Prince Albert? Since I am temporarily between engagements, we could set up a school of our own. I'll take out a provincial charter to establish the institution, and we'll call it the Louis Riel Memorial College of Chiropractic, Astrology, Basket-Weaving and Upholstery; Francis Z. Springer, Founder, President, Chairman of the Board, Dean of Women and Bursar; J.T. McLaughlin, Ph.D, Vice-President, Professor of Economics, and Chairman of the Parking Lot Committee. We could sell honourary doctorates to selected Ontario university presidents who lack them, and use as our superior, prestigious and more pricey award the degree of L.W.T., "Leader of Western Thought." With one of our diplomas or doctorates, plus a carefully filled out application, our graduates could qualify for unemployment insurance, entrance to Scientology short courses, or mental disability pensions. Real people and even politicians would line up to enrol. We'd clean up.

Think about it. I'm letting you in on a gold mine.

Collegially yours,

F.Z. Springer, L.W.T.

P.S.

Speaking of exercise and education, do you know any cure for the familiar and pervasive male complaint? I don't know how to put this, and maybe I've become intimidated a little by Stiffy's prowess, but lately I've been having a few problems. I've been sowing some wild oats, but recently experienced a few crop failures. My boomerang won't come back. Know what I mean? Probably it is all psychological, but we poor privates in the army of the unemployed occasionally have problems in saluting and presenting arms. This has never happened to me before. Stiffy thinks I'm joking, and keeps lining me up with his overflow of nurses, but the old hypodermic does not inject. Any advice?

Rather limply,

Z.

To: Francis Z. Springer
Prince Albert, Sask.

29 May 1977

Dear Zinger,

Gee, that's a heavy question. I have been told by medical scientists here that if you hang around the girls' gym, sniff bicycle seats, sit on hot water radiators, and subscribe to *Playboy*. . . .

Dear Zinger,

I'm certain that your problem is only fleeting and temporary. What I suggest is carving the taxidermically preserved vital parts off Mackenzie, frying them in olive oil, mixing them with Fleischman's Yeast and buffalo dung, and then when the moon is full. . . .

Dear Zinger,

Have you thought of yoga? I'm told there are yogis in the high Himalayas who can double forward on themselves like pretzels and, using the lips and the natural powers of ascendant spiritualism, perform wondrous acts of auto-erotic arousal as a preliminary to. . . .

Dear Zinger,

Take it easy, buddy. You are getting down on yourself needlessly. It's just that your spirits are a bit low and the situation seems bleak because of unemployment, but I've no doubt that Barney will ease you back onto the payroll in no time, and your Tiger Lily will soon be blooming again. Relax. Think about the higher philosophy, and why Gabriel Dumont with his cunning and his blunderbuss outsmarted the regiments with their imported Gatling gun. It's knowing the lie of the land that gets the bison. It's the cunning of the old warrior that wins the battle. When you are too pooped to cut the mustard, you can still lick the jar, but there can be no doubt that the old bull with his experience and his wiles is vastly superior to the crude young bucks who have no savvy and less control, who blunder about saying, "now this won't hurt a bit, did it?" They may be quick, but they have no staying power.

Not to worry, old friend. Things will soon be looking up. Focus your mind on more serious matters such as the founding of the College, the turning of the seasons, and the nature of the limerick, as well as the consolations of philosophy and of music. You are a champion and a selfless horn player in the Devil's dance band, Zinger, and don't let the violins swamp your brass. In any band, your trombone can always slide with the best of them. Damn the obligatos; let the dance go on. And even if you want to rest for a few bars, there's no harm in that. Oompahpah is always loud, but no substitute for the subtlety of the choice glissando.

Very best,

J.T.

From: Wilfred B. Twillington
Chiliast University Press

2 June 1977

Dear Professor McLaughlin,

I have some good news. When I sent your revised manuscript out for further review, I flagged it with a stamp of "urgent," and our mutual labours have quickly paid off.

Readers' reports are now in and unanimous, as well as enthusiastic, in recommending that your manuscript be accepted in its revised and now much more sophisticated form. Our assessors agreed that the pruning and editing which you performed this last round resulted in a work which is tight and well-focussed, greatly improved over the last version, and enormously superior to the preliminary draft which you submitted last autumn.

I am now in a position to offer you a contract to publish this undoubtedly useful and important work. Never before, since your adroit and sensitive revision, has the work of Innis so leapt from the page to convey the powerful meaning and inward subtlety of the thought of this great Canadian economist. Although your first draft lacked tight focus, and your second may have been rather discursive, this third draft effectively captures all the magic and penetrating insights of a major thinker, and now does credit to your own sharp analytic perceptions. Who can doubt that the scholarly editorial process, however prolonged and demanding, has but resulted in a manuscript which now does full justice to this important subject?

If you will be good enough to drop by our offices at your early convenience, our Mr. Williams says that he will be happy to discuss the nature of the publication agreement with you, and to have you sign, if you will be so kind, the required contract so that we can press on with printing with all dispatch. We like to get on with these details briskly, you understand.

Although you have from time to time pulled my leg about this project, I count it a distinct pleasure to have had the opportunity of working with you in honing and refining the manuscript. All's well that ends well, don't you think? I'm sure you now appreciate how the painful but inevitable process of scholarly editing has resulted in a vastly improved outcome, a product of which we have every reason to be proud.

What a pleasure it will be for me to see this book in print after all of the ardours of revision we have been through together.

Yours very sincerely,

Wilfred B. Twillington
Editor

To: Wilfred B. Twillington
Chiliast University Press

4 June 1977

Twilly old pal,

Terrific! Fantastic news. I always said you were a great guy, a superb editor, and a prince of a fellow altogether.

I'm delighted with the outcome, and have arranged with Williams to pop over on Thursday to sign the contract. I do hope you will be there so that we can renew our warm friendship. What would I have done without you, Twilly? I must say that your clear and penetrating editorial insights have been of inestimable value to me. Possibly this is why your letter makes it sound as though you did most of the work, but I'll still get my name on the cover too, won't I? Oh I do hope so. It means a lot to my old Mom.

Your friend,

J.T. McLaughlin

From: Spencer Tapsell,
Department of Economics,
University of Sask.

7 June 1977

J.T. Ol' Buddy,

There's *lots* of good news around lately, isn't there? Probably you have heard that I'm being made a Dean as of July. Now I won't have to set foot in a classroom for at *least* five years. Universities would be lovely places if it weren't for all those students. And Smig will be boosted to full professor in July as he has no doubt told you.

It was only the other day, though, that I met my friend Jimmy at a conference. He's the editor of *Canadian Economic History*. He tells me that an article of yours has been accepted by his journal and that it will be the lead piece in their autumn issue. Good for you. This may partially compensate you for the difficulties you've had with the book on Innis. Have you given up on that? If you had only heeded my advice the project would not have been so abortive.

Speaking of *dismal* failures, I was up in Prince Albert last week giving a talk to the Chamber of Commerce there ... it was very well received ... and I bumped into none other than that old mongrel Francis Z. Springer. He did not, I am sorry to say, apologize for his behaviour when last we met, but at least he summoned up the courtesy to congratulate me on my Deanship, so I decided to let bygones be bygones. I took him out for a night on the town, not that there's much flash in P.A. And I made a most laughable discovery.

Later in the evening, after some *serious* drinking (I was buying, on expense account, so the sauce flowed freely), I suggested that we pick up some chicks. Zinger didn't seem much interested, but kept his nose in the bottle. At the propitious moment there walked into the bar two little bimbos. I figured them for hookers right away. I told Zinger to sign them on, but he didn't budge. Just stared into his scotch like a boiled owl. Can't handle his liquor any more, by the way. So I just marched right up to them and said, "how'd you cute little dolls like to make bouncy-bouncy?" They were a bit slow off the mark until I gave them a gander at the old bank roll and riffled a fat pile of twenties, which got their attention I can *tell* you. So up we go to my room with Zinger trailing behind like a forlorn hound dog, and when we get to the room I get all unzipped but Z. makes no move. Just stands there. "What's with you, Zinger old boy?," I ask, but he doesn't even reply. He kept looking at me in the oddest way. I figured him just for blind drunk, when suddenly he blurts out something like, "I don't buy it and I can't stand it," and starts to leave. I pointed out to him that it was all paid for and there was no problem. Do you know what he did then? He said, "I've turned queer and I prefer clean boys to dirty goat Deans." Just like that. Then he walked out, without so much as a good-bye or a thank you.

Here's the discovery. I know as well as you know that whatever his hang-ups may be, and they seem to me many, Zinger is no queer. He was stringing me a line; I could tell that. And I've figured out what his problem really is. It was obvious once I thought about it. He's impotent. He's been drinking so long and so hard that he can't get it up. Isn't that a *hoot*?

When I got back to Saskatoon, naturally I passed this news along to Chappie. I assumed she'd be delighted. You know how women love revenge. Somehow, though, she seemed less amused by the news than I'd expected. She said almost nothing. Seemed to pout a bit. Strange girl. But I've no doubt she's quietly savouring it. Women – there's no understanding them.

Isn't that a helluva story? Imagine old Zinger, always trying to make out that he's a big man with the ladies, and his dong isn't dinging. What a chuckle. Thought I should share it with you.

I hope you and yours are well. Let me know how your work is going. Maybe Chiliast U. will keep you on another year on a temporary sessional basis on the strength of that article.

Keep on humping,

Spence

P.S.

Say, you never did tell me why in the world, if you ever had got that book out, you wanted Watkins to write the Foreword?

To: Spencer Tapsell,
Department of Economics,
University of Saskatchewan

10 June 1977

**TELEGRAM**

YOU ARE A VICIOUS AND UNBELIEVABLY VILE MORON STOP
YOU ARE A MEAN SCURVY SCUM STOP ALSO A FOUL AND
FETID LUMP OF FECAL MATTER FROM THE SOUTH END OF A
DISEASED CAMEL FACING NORTH STOP I PROMISE YOU THAT
WHEN NEXT WE MEET I WILL PUT POISON IVY IN YOUR
SHORTS AND HOPE THAT YOU DIE AN AGONIZING DEATH OF
TERMINAL JOCK ITCH STOP

J.T. MCLAUGHLIN

To: Jake Smigarowsky,
Department of Political Science
University of Saskatchewan

11 June 1977

Dear Smig,

That bastard Tapsell sent me a letter the other day that blew me away totally. He has reached new depths of meanness and depravity. I never would have believed it.

His only good news, which I wish you'd told me, is that you have reached the dizzy heights of full professorial rank. Good on you, Smig; I'm delighted. Warmest congratulations!

Yours truly is also feeling pretty good because this week I signed a contract with the Press and my book is now in the works. Things are looking very bright. Patricia almost cried when I told her, and I confess my heart went bumpety-bump. It was a long haul. Will you please mention this to Gandy? I'm eternally grateful to him. He made a suggestion a few weeks ago which I almost did not take seriously, but which proved to be dazzling. He'll tell you about it.

And undoubtedly Tapsell will have told you about Zinger. I suppose he's telling everybody. What a swine. Not only did he retail his grubby little story to me, but do you realize that he also told Chappie? My gawd! I fired off a telegram to the sonofabitch last night offering him my views on his character. The telegraph operator giggled and asked me whether the message was in code, but I think Spence will figure it out. Tell that turd that the next time he crosses my path he'd better be armed and well insured.

Tapsell also asked me why I wanted Mel Watkins to write a Foreword to my forthcoming great book. Have I not told you before my favourite story about Mel? Years ago when I was a teaching assistant and he was a very junior Lecturer, Mel and I were assigned to teach elementary economics to hordes of engineers in a huge and crowded theater seating 250 students. It wasn't an easy teaching assignment, and what made it worse was that the class met at 1:00 P.M., the time when the students wanted to eat. Can you imagine lecturing to a mob of 250 louts all stuffing their faces at the same time? Watkins announced that he couldn't stand it, and that eating in class was not allowed. The boys explained to him that they had other classes that day right through from 9:00 A.M. till 1:00, plus compulsory labs all afternoon. They had no other time in which they could possibly eat, they said. Mel remained firm: no eating during the lecture. They persisted in their objections, but Mel hung tough. Finally one bold youth exclaimed to Watkins, "After all, sir, man must eat to live!" Quick as a wink Mel shot back, "Yes, and procreate the species too, but NOT in my class."

Always had a soft spot for Watkins after that.

Best regards,

J.T.

From: Francis Z. Springer,
Prince Albert, Sask.

15 June, '77

J.T.,

One of the neighbour boys put it to me the other day. It seemed a little too close to the knuckle.

Question: What is warm and brown and crawls up your leg?
Answer: Homesick shit.

Only difference is, I'm home and Chappie isn't. You know, J.T., I really miss that broad. She's got a tongue on her like a cat-o'-nine-tails, and patient she is not, but she was always spicy and feisty. It's not the same without her. What were you telling me earlier about the old hearts and flowers crap? I may yet be reduced to that. Whatever.

What I wanted to tell you is, Dowie has gone south for a few weeks and Barney has re-hired me. I'm back on the job again. When we open our College, I may be ready to teach courses in journalism (as if it could be learned), such as "How to Maintain Job Security," and "How to Write Profound Editorials in 14 Minutes." Not to mention "The Place of the Limerick in Writing Obituaries."

Before I went back to the city desk, however, I took up your challenge concerning the backwards limerick. It is less easy to do than it seems, I agree. But never will a Springer accept defeat. Stiffy and I beguiled an evening in a pub recently and applied our formidable intellects to the challenge.

Any fool knows that the Thurber example is unsatisfactory because inadequately scatological. As the immortal Don Marquis said, there are limericks to be told when ladies are present, limericks to be told when ladies have withdrawn and clergymen are present, and LIMERICKS. We have devoted our attention to the latter genre, the real thing. Such as:

> A soupey old turtle of mock
> Had a schlong like a buster of block;
>   This hell of a rake
>   Wooed an elle name of Raque,
> But she welched, as do teasers of cock.

If that is too far out for you, we offer this alternative modification:

> A randy old turtle of mock
> Had a prick like a buster of block;
>   In a chowder of fish
>   he could not shun co-ish
> and frigged up ta puss name of Oc.

Or with a little polishing we might serve up something along these lines:

> An ilever whose penis was cant,
> Orphaned, knew his asm was phant;
>   "Mon quoi, je ne sais,
>   As a ward, there's no way."
> Avoiding cousins, he mounted his tante.

Somehow I'm not convinced that the CBC would buy a whole program along these lines, but it helps to pass the time.

How is your work going? Why don't you attempt a book of fiction or even humour if you can't make a go of Innis? Economics is O.K., I guess, but I always thought you capable of something more. You are too timid.

Come visit me. My spirits are still not high.

> Regards,
>
> Zinger

To: Francis Z. Springer,
Prince Albert, Sask.

18 June 1977

Zinger!

I got it! I'm home and dry. This morning I received a phone call from my Chairman. I'd had a talk with him ten days ago, showing him my contract, all signed, sealed and delivered, to publish my epic book on Innis. It's going to be in print! I'm going to be a big-assed strutting author of an honest-to-God book. I handed the Chairman this dirty-great official contract with forests of fine print and the signature of the senior editor of the Press. I also laid on him a note from the editor of *Canadian Economic History*, accepting my article on Innis and McLuhan which I'd culled from the book, and undertaking to pay me the princely sum of $50 for the reprint rights as well as providing a free subscription to the journal. How's that for wealth and fame and glory?

Anyway, the Chairman agreed to re-submit my curriculum vitae and revised publication record to the Departmental Tenure Committee and, wonder of wonders, Manticore of the Fifth Business, I have been awarded tenure. Think of it. Tenure! God how I've sweated and prayed for it. Now it's a reality. Not only that, but I also get promotion to the rank of Associate Professor, plus a salary increase. I've got it in writing. With this raise, I'll be making almost as much as a plumber or a TV repair man.

But it's what I've always wanted, Zinger. I'm in clover. Patricia is relieved and very happy.

You've got your job back. I've got my job locked up. Let us rejoice, therefore, O my brother, and make a glad noise unto the Lord. When I come out west in July I'm going to buy you the biggest fucking steak in Prince Albert, and maybe buy a half-interest in your college. I figure we can't miss, laddy. You and me against the world, and we're winners, Zinger, winners! Employment. Tenure. What more could we ask of this improbable and whimsical world?

Euphorically,

J.T. (L.W.T.)

From: Margot Chapman Springer,
Saskatoon, Saskatchewan

20 June 1977

J.T. old dear,

You've been a brick about my problems and marital difficulties – meddlesome and obstreperous, but pretty decent. I appreciate your friendship.

Recently I have received rather disturbing news from a strange source concerning Zinger's health. I wanted you to know, because you seem to care about and hang in with Francis Z., that although I have been outraged by much of his recent behaviour, and sometimes would like to carve off his balls for earrings, I have been touched by his apparent repentance and some poems he sent me recently, as well as by reports that his physical health is somewhat imperfect. His mental health, God knows, will never be up to standard, but I really hate to think of him suffering physically.

I may have to rethink this whole thing from the bottom line. Young John tells me that he misses some of his pals in Prince Albert. It hasn't been altogether easy for me here in Saskatoon, but I guess life isn't simple anywhere. What I'm trying to say is that nothing is final yet. It's hard, but I'm trying to shift, with much clanking and grinding of emotional gears. Do you, since I know you are always in touch with him, have any reason to believe that Zinger has any difficulties or health problems that he's not telling me about?

I've got to admit that sometimes he worries me. The big lug is really not all bad, you know that? His rude bellowing does not conceal a lot of – other things.

Very best,

Chappie

To: Margot Chapman Springer,
Saskatoon, Saskatchewan

25 June 1977

**TELEGRAM**

HAVE REASON TO BELIEVE ZINGER IS IN DESPERATE SHAPE
STOP NOT SURE THAT HE CAN KEEP HIS JOB OR HIS SANITY
WITHOUT YOU STOP HE TELLS ME EVERY WEEK THAT HIS
WORLD WENT DARK WHEN YOU WALKED OUT STOP HIS
PHYSICIANS INFORM ME THAT THERE IS SOME DOUBT ABOUT
HIS FUTURE UNLESS HE REGAINS EMOTIONAL KEEL STOP
EARNESTLY SUGGEST THAT YOU BE IN TOUCH WITH HIM
SOONEST AND CLOSEST IF HE IS TO BE SALVAGED STOP HIS
NEED IS GREAT AND URGENT STOP ONLY YOU COMMA
CHAPPIE ONLY YOU STOP

J.T. MCLAUGHLIN

To: Margot Chapman Springer,
Saskatoon, Saskatchewan

25 June 1977

Dear Chappie,

After firing off that telegram earlier tonight, and after a few more midnight thoughts about what it all might mean, I confess I don't really know what to say about all this.

My fear is that Zinger may be in danger of some kind of a breakdown. He is not well. I have the strong sense that he's in pretty ropey shape. You are needed, Chappie, really needed by that man.

We know that he's irrepressible and a survivor, a tough turkey who will not let the bastards get him down. But will he get, has he got, himself down? Can he stand being alone? Can anyone?

I really believe that he can do his own improbable thing only if he has the security and the rudder that you and you alone provide. Probably he can't ever stop his capering, but he needs – what we all need – indulgence and forgiveness, plus the reassurance of the tender loving snare. I believe you are the prize in his box of Crackerjacks, his lottery ticket and his hope, his port in the storm. He has his freedom and his fun; what he lacks is happiness.

I know this whole thing isn't easy for you. If you need to be on your own for a bit longer, or even forever, gawd knows your friends will understand. But will you be able to look into your mailbox without the niggling hope that there will be a letter from Zinger?

With love,

J.T.

From: Margot Chapman Springer,
Saskatoon

29 June 1977

J.T. old dear,

Your telegram and following letter joggled me into making further inquiries about the man I used to be – well, still am – married to, and all reports seem to confirm that he isn't in flourishing good spirits or the best of health. Sometimes I think, "who cares?," and sometimes he almost makes me weep.

I'm trying to rethink this, seriously. In spite of everything, I care about him, and yet I'm not sure I could reverse my earlier decision to go it alone. To you I'll admit that the life of the single working woman, with young John to consider, is no bed of petunias. Oh, I can hack it, but there are days, and nights, when I question whether I've made the right decision. Loneliness is a stark fact. One does get the dreads, you know? There are times when I think I may be leaning too hard on young John, emotionally depending on him too much.

And, recently Zinger sent me some poems. Did I tell you that? Not another dead duck, not limericks, but poems. I was, well, surprised. He'll never change, of course, not fundamentally. Still, you've got to give old Francis Z. one thing; he isn't boring.

God but I've met some men in Saskatoon who are bores. Earnest and nice, but so – predictable. When you get down to it, one of the basic questions is, what could you possibly say to a guy who shows up for a date wearing a three-piece suit? They're grubby little ants, mostly, and I guess I have a perverse predilection for grasshoppers.

Not that I'd ever be able to abide the dopey antics of Zinger, you understand. He's a damned fool; we all know that.

I realize what you want me to do. You mean well. But it's MY life that's at stake. Surely you appreciate that this is the only life I've got to live, and I could do something different with it. That isn't entirely selfish, is it? I could make choices, J.T., real choices. I could move to Vancouver, or Calgary, or anywhere.

But to you, I suppose, my choices must seem few and simple. Stay or go; return or flee. I wish it were that simple.

You must have a strange view of all this. I mean, as his oldest friend, presumably you do not regard Zinger simply as a mad gazoonie who should be written off and forgotten. Neither do I, I guess. But how do you understand him, how could you explain him? Do you consider him just a raunchy hyperbolic and hyperballsy adolescent who cannot, will not, grow up? An overgrown, if not entirely lovable kid who refuses to accept what the world calls "responsibility?" (Kid, hell – he's forty-one!) Or do you see him as a forlorn figure, something of a pathetic hero, who long ago set his own rules, however narrow and selfish, and is too proud and stubborn to admit amendment or defeat? Possibly you've never shifted or sharpened your view of him since high school. I never know which of his lies you believe, or which he may half believe himself. Knowing his delusions, do you patronize and pity him? Or do you, I sometimes wonder, want to believe him – and even envy him? In a sense, he is a free individual, and untamable, damn him. There aren't many of those left in the world. How do you see him? Tell me.

But to me, the choices are more difficult. Even from the perspective of our separation, I regard him as – oh, I don't know – as a liability, an exasperation, a father, a debtor, an ogre, a clown, a husband, a failure, a triumph, a glorious aberration, a horse's ass, an impossible egoist, a little boy, an anarchist, a cherished enemy, an infuriating friend. He's been a barnacle on my keel, but sometimes also a fresh wind in my sail.

And I'm becalmed. I guess I'm feeling shipwrecked. For me on this arid sea of the imponderable prairie, no stirring breeze blows, no chinook brings promise of warmth or ease or gentle rain.

I'm damned if I know what to do, J.T., double damned.

Next week I may, I'm not sure, I may try to have another talk to him when my classes and marking are finished. Much as I like the students, it isn't clear whether I have the guts to be a teacher for the

rest of my life. Teaching is tough. That much at least you'll understand.

So, what to do about Zinger? The mind clicks, but the heart tugs.
Probably I'll have to give weight to the factor of his precarious health;
I don't much like some of the things I've heard on that score. Anyway, the instinct for self-preservation was never my long suit, or I'd
never have married the big ape in the first place.

Love,

Chappie

To: Margot Chapman Springer,
Saskatoon

3 July 1977

Dear Chappie,

What can I say? I can't make up your mind for you. I can't even
honestly answer your questions as to how I see Zinger. To me he
isn't a problem, but a fact and a friend. Maybe I don't "see" him at
all; maybe I just enjoy him from a discreet distance as an immutable
fact of nature, a hot geyser like Old Faithful, a spurting eruption
from down below where Jung says we live, reminding me of where I
came from and what I once hoped before I became enmeshed in the
coils of mortgages and tenure and academe.

All I can say is, follow your heart. Do what you have to do. I
certainly hope . . . but I've said all that before. It's your yellow brick
road, Chappie, and no one but you can choose the turnings.

May your slippers be magic.

Love from Trish and

J.T.

P.S.

My daughter Jossy has a T-shirt with a slogan I like. It says: "Give
Someone a Hug Today."

From: Francis Z. Springer,
Prince Albert, Sask.

3 July, '77

J.T.

Congratulations on your tenure. A tiresome and tawdry trinket to be sure, a trifling ticket to temenos twee turpitude treasured typically by timorous Torontonians, but congratulations none the less. You seem to care about that sort of thing, although I am still at a loss to know why. Boy scout badges are all very nice if you have a boy scout mentality. Whatever.

Things are also looking up a bit here in P.A. Chappie actually phoned me the other night, just as though I were a real human being. It was good to talk to her, proper bitch that she often is. Our strained silence of some months has now been broken, but I doubt me whether she is after much other than increased alimony. Women.

You didn't tell me how you liked the reverse limericks? Stiffy and I are still working on them, and contemplating a surpassingly venal and meretricious application for a Canada Council grant if we can pull enough of them together to make a book. If those artsy assholes in Ottawa would only realize it, the limerick is a far more flourishing art form than the short story or the opera, and more deserving of financial support, but I'm sure that the usual eastern discrimination against qualified western applicants would prevent us being seriously considered for a handout. We intend to apply, but the Canada Council seems to me a conspiratorial cabal of Toronto-Ottawa commuters and culpably clueless cretins.

Anyway, Stiffy and I were hoisting a draught or three the other night when he contrived the interesting notion of paying a return visit to the hospital. He was very happy there. Wanted to renew acquaintances. I myself had a slight but salubrious bit of a fling recently with a frisky nurse who works there, so I phoned ahead and instructed her to dust off her pussy and get down to the front door to meet us.

The salacious and slavering welcoming committee for Stiffy you wouldn't have believed. Among the nurses he seems firmly established as a local hero if not a national monument. Hectic hearts and baby-doll nighties were all aflutter when we arrived.

Armed with an extra quart each of Old Infuriator, Stiffy and I made a grand tour of the nurses' residence and favoured the assembled multitude with a few musical selections from the classical repertoire such as "The Indian Love Call" and "Auntie Mary had a Canary up the Leg of her Drawers." We then ventured into the hospital itself, the scene of many of Stiffy's recent tribulations and triumphs.

"These corridors," he announced, "being long and marble-floored, are ideally suited to white-man's indoor games." "Such as what?" I inquired, with characteristic innocence. "Such as curling. I'm sure I'd enjoy curling. Apparently it is a game much relished by you palefaces." "But Stiffy, we do not have any curling stones. What will we use?" "No problem," he responded, "we will employ bed-pans. They make admirable substitutes for curling rocks." Whereupon he reached into a cupboard and clattered down a huge pile of these fundamental utensils and began gleefully to cast them down the corridor of the geriatric ward. "Sweep!" he implored, and two obliging nurses, enthusiastically entering into the spirit of the event, threw off their uniforms and began using them to sweep in the van of the sliding pans. Nursing costumes make excellent brooms and also, when removed and devoted to athletic endeavour, reveal edifying expanses of jiggly pink flesh. At this point several rickety old citizens emerged from their rooms amid the din and cheered for the curling skipper of their choice. Wagers were offered and covered. Nurses were exhorted and uncovered. Bottles were passed from hand to hand to refresh both players and spectators. Tits bounced and bed-pans clashed and skimmed as we got down to it for serious stakes. Nurse Higgins made book. You'd be surprised how diverting curling can be in such circumstances. I haven't had so much fun since

Dowie caught his finger in the printing press last winter.

I believe we may have caused a bit of a commotion, if not a small noise, because within minutes of our game reaching full cry and the cheerleaders performing cartwheels, there appeared in our corridor-rink a number of censorious and ill-tempered medical authorities who ranted and raved a fair bit, gesticulated wildly, and conveyed the distinct impression that they preferred our game should be terminated.

"Not bloody likely," said Stiffy, "my team is ahead eight pans to six, and that old party there in the kimono, clicking his teeth and throwing off his truss, is about to cast his poopoo-platter at the big circle for the top prize, a weekend at Lake Katepwa with Nurse Higgins." Higgins, a well-rounded and toothsome lass, then emitted a squeal of delight, loosened the knot of her long hair, and sat in a pan which Stiffy immediately propelled down the hall via a brisk shove with a crutch. "Whee!" cried Nurse Higgins, sliding merrily along. "Hooray!" shouted the canny wagerer who had laid even odds on her left buttock touching home base. "Crazy," observed Stiffy as he grasped another frolicksome slider and sat her in a pan to use as the next projectile.

I think it was at this point that there appeared a most formidable old gorgonzola, the Head Nurse, none other than the distempered and decidedly disagreeable virago who earlier had bedevilled my Indian friend with excessive rectal attentions during his stay in the hospital. She was in curlers, bathrobe, disarray and some high dudgeon. At first, being somewhat befuddled by firewater, Stiffy did not recognize her. Taking another swig from his quart of Old Infuriator, Stiffy contemplated the loud interloper with benign curiosity. Pensively scratching his nuts and regarding her like a fat bug under a microscope, he inquired, "Wayna way owha, keeyaka shisk?" Translated freely from the Cree, his question meant, "Who is this itchy asshole?"

Their gazes met, and you could tell they did not regard each other cordially. Liberty had met Authority; devilish delight had encountered dread decorum. The old biddy, utilizing a surprisingly strong side-arm curve-ball delivery, flung a bed-pan at the head of my intrepid friend, then rushed down the hall screaming that she'd call the cops. This disconcerting and gratuitous act of violence seemed to spark in Stiffy some belated glimmer of inebriated recognition. Instantly he went wahooing after her, eyes wild with homicidal intent. She fled. He yelped and pursued, giving vent to fearsome warlike native cries which I think he'd learned from old John Wayne movies. War whoops. Bellows of anguish and dismay. They disappeared around a corner in full frenzy, leaving several disbelieving patients, a gaggle of giggling dishevelled nurses, and your obedient servant clutching the bottles of hooch against unseemly spillage.

When Stiffy returned he had the old broad, bathrobe up and bum foremost, gagged and strapped face down on a rolling bed, a wheeled stretcher, which he shoved along before him. A cheerful grin suffused his countenance. "What are you doing with her," I inquired, trying to make conversation. "Why do you have her trussed up and face down like that?" "I'm taking her temperature," replied Stiffy with dignity, "just as she used to do with me. Rectally." "With a daffodil?" I asked. "Yes," he said, "do unto others."

Pausing to rest, Stiffy regarded his handiwork with evident satisfaction. "Does anyone here happen to possess a tattooing needle?" he wondered. Unhappily, none of us had such an implement about our persons. "Pity," he mused; "I might have inscribed upon her vast hind cheek some suitable slogan as a memento of the occasion. Something like 'Red Power' or 'Remember Batoche.' My god, she has an ass as big as Prince Edward Island, doesn't she? Gulley Jimson could paint a mural on it. Perhaps, lacking more artistic instruments, I could replace that somewhat wilted daffodil with the vigorous insertion of, say, a turnip?" Again, a search through our pockets revealed a plentiful lack of appropriate vegetables of any description. The best I could offer was a roll of Lifesavers which, being butterscotch, Stiffy declined.

"No matter," he sighed. "Fortunately my esteemed ancestors have bequeathed to me extensive supernatural powers." "Stiffy, you wouldn't!" Nurse Higgins squealed. "Tut, tut, bloody tut," came the disdainful reply. "Nothing indecorous. I merely mean that I have a firm grounding in the ancient arts of the Medicine Man. If you will be so good as to stand back and give me room, I shall now hurl myself into a ritual Medicine Dance and chant wondrous imprecations and incantations which will enable me to transform yonder white-assed shrew into a buffalo." And so saying, he began to yip and caper and cavort in a most astonishing manner. "What do you call that dance?" I inquired. "Swan Lake, it ain't." "No," puffed Stiffy, "it's not Swan Lake, but more of a Prairie-Chicken Slough, or mayhap The Dance of the Sugar Plum Furies. Traditional stuff, you know."

It was about then that the Royal Canadian Mounted, doubtless torn away from opening mail and performing other nefarious covert duties to protect the common weal, arrived to police up the joint. Some consternation ensued. Recognizing the awkwardness of the situation, several of Stiffy's undraped nurse friends threw themselves on the Horsemen, panting "My saviour, my hero," creating a useful diversion and permitting us time to escape before we encountered unwelcome questions or circumstances which might have involved handcuffs. Speedily, and through the hedges, we made our separate ways home. Given the rather bare condition of some of the prime witnesses, the Mounties seemed in no great hurry to leave and pursue, which suited me just as well, since I am still on probation from the alleged ostrich offence. Thus did the raunchy redskin's devoted fan club help to preserve our civil liberties. There may have been a bit of damage, but I guess it's all covered by Medicare and nothing serious, unless that damn daffodil was thrust up as far as the Head Nurse's epiglottis. I rather hope so.

Altogether it was an exhilarating evening.

Wish you'd been here.

Zinger

To: Francis Z. Springer,
Prince Albert, Sask.

7 July 1977

Dear Zinger,

Your improbable tale of the nocturnal visit to the hospital takes the cake for imagination and hyperbole. I don't believe much of it. Still, your real or imaginary exploits lead me to conclude that you have overcome your temporary affliction and regained your physical, ah, composure.

Things are looking up with me, too. I don't know when I've felt so content or at peace with the world. Cutty and I have accepted an advance of $1,000 each from a publisher for our textbook. Patricia is off buying new dresses, and we have paid the camp bills for the kids' summer. With tenure achieved and a book on the way, plus a text-book at the printer's, things are pretty rosy. I'm thinking of visiting my mother later in July, then stopping off with Smig in Saskatoon, and maybe dropping in on you in Prince Albert for a day or two. How does that strike you?

Having calmed down now after the tenure triumph, I'm beginning to wonder if it's what I really want in the long run. I'm thinking of writing to the University of Lethbridge and applying for a position there which I heard might still be open. Alternatively, I might change my profession entirely and become a lion tamer, or perhaps a teapot.

Do send me advice.

Long may your pole vault.

J.T.

From: Francis Z. Springer,
Prince Albert, Sask.

11 July, '77

J.T.,

Yeah, things could be worse. You should indeed take a crack at Lethbridge or any opening in the west. Anything to escape the preening pretensions of Toronto. Whatever.

Personally, I'm feeling decidedly frisky in the warm summer weather, and still on the right side of the jail-house door. All systems are go. The Head Nurse decided not to press charges, presumably because she did not much want to testify in open court as to all of the up-thrust details of our evening's jollity at the hospital. Maybe she's a curling fan.

Things are also running middling well at the office, and I managed to persuade Barney to give Nurse Higgins a reporting job on the paper. She has been finding life at the hospital rather dull lately, and wants to try writing, as well as being closer to Stiffy.

That worthy rascal has had another spot of good luck. After considering what you'd said about his car, he placed an ad in a U.S. antique automobile magazine to test the market, with a picture of his unlikely vehicle, and he has received a lot of bids, including an offer of $50,000 from a collector in Arizona who is coming up next week. Stiffy says to thank you, and has promised to hold out for $55,000 before he parts with the Pungs-Finch, the extra 5 Gs being a commission for me, wise and deserving fellow that I am. My cup runneth over.

But you know, much as I enjoy Stiffy and other friends, I sort of miss Chappie. She's more fun to fight with than anyone else. To tell the whole truth, the world is more than a little flat and stale with me some nights. Chappie persists in playing sillybuggers, but I hope she'll soon knock off with the charade. All life, of course, is a crazy game played by fools on a dung-heap, a game of which we never learn all the rules and hazards till it's too late. We play at being both the hunter and the hunted; trouble is, we seldom know when we're being which. But this Snakes and Ladders bit is a good romp, and amusing, so long as you don't commit the sin of solemnity.

Some nights, though, are harder than others. I must admit that there are times when even my spavined ass drags a bit. There are days when I guffaw at your curious quest for tenure, but there are also days when I don't like work, and I don't like being unemployed. Times when I don't like being drunk, but don't like being sober. Often I can't take being alone, and can't stand company. Recently I've known evenings when I don't feel like going to bed early, but am not sure I can bear being awake.

Maybe I should try writing a novel. That seems terribly easy, and mildly diverting. Don't you think I could win a Pulitzer?

Yours from upsy-downsy land,

Zinger

From: Margot Chapman Springer,
Prince Albert, Sask.

15 July 1977

J.T. old dear,

Note the address above. That it should come full circle to this! Here's how it happened.

I was a bit worried by stories I'd heard about Zinger, and I suppose on the whole I found life on my own in Saskatoon less beguiling than I'd hoped. Anyway, on the weekend I found myself driving with John back to Prince Albert to see how things were with Francis Z. When I arrived at the house I found nobody here, and spent a short while cleaning and tidying up the place, from sheer force of habit, I guess. But when I went back out to the car I found that its wheels were gone. Not just the tires, but the entire wheels! Can you pawn automotive stuff? Presumably. The inimitable journalist had struck again, a classic "gottcha." There was even a characteristic note on the windshield, saying: "If you need a new car, phone your friendly local Studebaker dealer." I raged. I wept. I even laughed. Predictably, I'd been had.

However, it was clear that John was glad to be back in the house and in P.A. I confess not all of it felt bad to me. Much later, after I'd had a long heart-to-heart with Zinger, I discovered that he'd filched and hidden my purse, with everything in it including my cheque book, so I couldn't leave town if I'd wanted to unless I was prepared to set off hitch-hiking at midnight.

Therefore.

I'm here.

But God only knows, J.T., what will become of us all. I feel like Laocoon wrestling with the serpents. Shortly after I returned, and I must admit Zinger was unusually pleasant and glad to see me, the damned fool did it again.

He got fired. Dowie has given him the shove. It seems that a well known salesman for a local brewery, one Chuggalug Charlie Chalmers, died over the weekend and Barney told Zinger to prepare an obituary. He did, but at the last minute, and managed to slide in to the piece what he called "Charlie's favourite poem":

> There was a young girl named Anhauser
> Who swore that no man could surprise her;
> But Pabst took a chance,
> Found a Schlitz in her pants,
> And now she is sadder – Budweiser.

So Zinger is unemployed again. I may need your moral support, or a Care package, or my head read. Clearly I'm back where I started, the proud possessor of a car with no wheels and a husband with no sense. Things are not tranquil, but neither are they dull. I keep telling myself, it's better than marking exams. So is a kick in the head with a frozen boot.

Damned if I know which way to turn or what to do. I feel as though I were back in a padded cell. Still, it may be better than exile.

I'll keep in touch, if God and Francis Z. spare me and I am not carted off to jail on a murder rap.

Very best to you and yours,

Chappie

From: Francis Z. Springer,
Prince Albert, Sask.

17 July, '77

J.T.,

I have news. Big but not surprising news. Chappie is back in the fold. We have patched things up. Always knew she'd see reason and come home. I have romanced and sweet-talked her until her heart melted in the hot furnace of my irresistible blandishments.

She moved back in last weekend, and seems quite contrite. But you know me, always willing to forgive and forget. It's nice to have her around; the meals are better, and now I feel less pressure to find a replacement for Mackenzie. Today Chappie found a slot in one of the local schools for the fall, so she'll be teaching here in P.A. and the extra income will be handy in case we decide to take up major philanthropical works. It's also pleasant to have young John back in the house. Lately I've noticed signs that he may be moving from the chaos of adolescence into the major bewilderment of adulthood, and it's very satisfying to watch his puzzled progress. Thank God he has a pillar of sense in me to lean on.

I've decided, on reflection, to take a short leave of absence from work. Might even quit, and let them try to struggle along without me. I've told Stiffy that when his Arizona ship comes in from the Pungs-Finch we should pool our immense financial resources and make a takeover bid to buy the paper. Probably we could buy it cheap after Dowie runs it into the ground in my absence.

Anyway, I'm treating the family to an outing and taking us all up to Candle Lake for a little holiday. Chappie may need the rest. So you won't be hearing from me for a while. I'll drop you a postcard later in the summer, but I suspect the mailman needs a holiday too, and all of us here look forward to a quiet space. As I told Barney when he protested that he couldn't handle all the editorials alone, I've left (with my renowned foresight and efficiency) an extra large pile of writing for page six that he can run A.O.T., Any Old Time. A.O.T. is my favourite schedule. Whatever.

As Willie-the-Lion Smith used to say, "I hate to leave you, but I'm gonna depart slow, and come back real quick."

Whack your porcupine,<br>
and twiddle your tenure.

Zinger

P.S.

By the way, Chappie said a curious thing last night when Tapsell's name came up. She said I should not bad-mouth Spence, but should really be grateful to him. Then she clammed up. Why him, of all people? You don't suppose she had a thing going with him in Saskatoon, do you? Nah, I guess that's too far out. Not to worry, I always say. It's all shitteroo. Zing it.

Love to all,

Z.